How to Develop Your Child's Gifts and Talents During the Elementary Years

How to Develop Your Child's Gifts and Talents During the Elementary Years

♦ ♦ ♦

by RaeLynne P. Rein, Ph.D. and Rachel Rein

Lowell House
Los Angeles
....
Contemporary Books
Chicago

Library of Congress Cataloging-in-Publication Data

Rein, RaeLynne Pellinger.
    How to develop your child's gifts and talents during the
elementary years / RaeLynne P. Rein and Rachel Rein.
        p.   cm.
    Includes bibliographical references.
    ISBN 1-56565-165-0
    1. Child development.   2. Child rearing.   3. Self-realization.
I. Rein, Rachel.   II. Title.
HQ767.9.R45   1994
649'.124—dc20   94-30149
                                                   CIP

Requests for such permissions should be addressed to:

> Lowell House
> 2029 Century Park East, Suite 3290
> Los Angeles, CA 90067

Lowell House books can be purchased at special discounts when ordered in bulk for
premiums and special sales. Contact Department VH at the above address.

Publisher: Jack Artenstein
General Manager: Elizabeth Duell Wood
Editorial Director: Brenda Pope-Ostrow
Director of Publishing Services: Mary D. Aarons
Illustrations: Larry Nolte
Text Design: Judy Doud Lewis
Cover Design: Lisa-Theresa Lenthall

Manufactured in the United States of America
10 9 8 7 6 5 4 3 2 1

———

To Adam Rein and
Raymond T. Pellinger,
with all our love

———

Acknowledgments

We would like to thank the following people for
their suggestions and help on this project:
Margaret Briggs, Howard Gershan, Hap Palmer, Robert Rein,
and especially our fearless editor, Brenda Pope-Ostrow.

◆ ◆ ◆

We would also like to thank the following individuals who so
graciously gave of their time to be interviewed:
Steve Allen, Carol Halperin, Linda Havard,
Hap Palmer, and Susan Silbert.

Contents

Introduction 9

Chapter One
Identifying Your Child's Gifts and Talents 13

Chapter Two
The Gift of Leadership 23

Chapter Three
The Gift of Creativity 45

Chapter Four
The Gift of Social Consciousness 75

Chapter Five
The Gift of Humor 111

Chapter Six
Answers to Common Questions
About Gifts, Talents, and Interests 131

Notes 141

Introduction

When I found I had crossed
that line, I looked at my hands
to see if I was the same person.
There was such a glory over
everything; the sun came
like gold through the trees, and
over the fields, and I felt like I
was in Heaven. [1]

Harriet Tubman,
American abolitionist

Ten-year-old Margaret is not particularly popular with her peers. She is an outstanding artist who especially loves to draw portraits of her family.

Jason is a cheerful eight-year-old who is having a little trouble keeping up in his math class. He's got a big heart and is tremendously kind and considerate. He wants to be a doctor when he grows up.

Christine is reading on a fourth-grade level, two years ahead of most of her classmates. She's also the star of her soccer team. Her mother has noticed, however, that she has trouble controlling her temper when she is playing with her friends.

Leroy, a spirited fifth grader, has excellent social skills. In fact, he has more friends than he can handle. Academically, he functions on an average level.

◆　◆　◆

What do these children have in common?
They all have special areas of interest, strengths, gifts, and talents that can be nurtured and encouraged.

P arents genuinely want their children to develop to their fullest potential. In fact, a parent's primary objective is to help her or his youngster develop specific gifts, talents, and interests. Unfortunately, many parents, even the most enlightened and educated, do not know how to accomplish this very basic and all-important goal.

In *How to Develop Your Child's Gifts and Talents During the Elementary Years*, our purpose is to provide you with a guide to nurturing your child's gifts and talents in a joyous and effective manner. By recognizing and encouraging your child's individual interests and strengths, not only will you help develop her or his essential critical and creative thinking abilities, but you will also help your child lead a more fulfilling life. As a parent, your involvement is crucial. Although there is a growing debate as to just how much parents can and should influence their children's development[2], the prevailing view from child psychologists and educators is that the behavior of parents has a significant impact on the emotional and intellectual functioning of their daughters and sons.

The preschool years are a time for sensory stimulation, general development, movement exploration, and play experiences. The primary concern of parents during this period should be to provide young children with a wide variety of social, educational, physical, and moral experiences. Most children in this age range are like sponges, and with the appropriate levels of guidance and exposure, they learn remarkably quickly.

During the elementary school years, *all* children are manifesting areas of strength, personality traits, topics of interest, and specific skills that parents can identify and help develop. Some of these areas may lead children to socialize with like-minded friends. Others may influence their decisions on what courses to take in high school and college. Still others may have a direct impact on future career plans. There are also those abilities and interests that will be relatively short-lived. But whatever the outcome, children's gifts and talents deserve to be recognized and encouraged. These talents bring joy to youngsters and are the perfect vehicles for optimizing learning and growth.

This book focuses on the elementary school years, grades one through five, and is designed to be user-friendly. In Chapter One, several suggestions are provided in the form of four steps that set the foundation for developing a child's strengths. These steps emphasize how to identify gifts and talents. Chapters Two through Five cover specific areas of strength your child may demonstrate. Among the many gifts and talents that can be nurtured, in the interests of space this book examines four: leadership, creativity, social consciousness, and humor. Included in each chapter are several activities that you can do with your child, such as games, discussion topics, and hobbies; community resources to be tapped; current relevant research findings; where to go for more information in specific areas; and interviews with adults whose families have successfully encouraged and nurtured their particular strengths and interests.

The process of raising children does not always run smoothly. Chapter Six provides answers to commonly asked questions concerning gifts, talents, and interests, including how to handle interests that appear to be excessive or inappropriate. Also included are helpful suggestions on how to use interests, gifts, and talents to improve your child's areas of weakness.

So jump in, and happy parenting!

Identifying Your Child's Gifts and Talents

Parents have become so
convinced that educators know
what is best for children that
they forget that they themselves
are really experts. [3]

Marian Wright Edelman,
American founder and president of the
Children's Defense Fund

Step 1:
Assume that all children have special gifts and talents.

An increasingly popular belief in the field of psychology holds that there are multiple intelligences or areas of talent in which individuals can excel.[4] With this in mind, we can assume that all children possess gifts, talents, strengths, and areas of special interest. Every youngster, from the most disabled to the highest achieving, has one or more special qualities, skills, or characteristics. Once this assumption is fully embraced with all the resolve and determination that can be mustered, then the process of parenting takes on an unending, joyful quality.

This approach can be tricky, since our society tends to categorize and label children. Does the term *hyperactive* sound familiar? How about *mentally retarded, autistic, difficult, creative, shy,* or maybe *a loner*? Although words are necessary to communicate, once a child is labeled, all the behavior that is seen, plus the total of who that child is, stems from the framework of that particular label. To complicate matters, language not only reflects one's thinking, it also helps shape the way people think. Thus, a self-perpetuating cycle is formed. For example, Johnny is (fill in the blank) because he behaves this way. Johnny behaves this way because he is (fill in the blank).

In actuality, children are incredibly complex and interesting individuals. Parents do young people a great disservice by viewing them in a narrow light, especially one imposed on them by others. Once a child's richness and individuality are acknowledged, however, the parent/child relationship is opened and expanded in a healthy way, and children can blossom before their parents' eyes. Furthermore, once parents believe that every child is gifted and talented, then even the most seemingly average child takes on a whole new look. It is important to stress that there is nothing wrong with being "average." We aren't trying to get you to mold your children into something they are not, nor are we trying to get you to mold your children into what you want them to be. Rather, when you look openly and carefully at your children, you will see so much more than average. The key is to recognize that all children have strengths, and to learn to utilize those strengths as a foundation for growth.

The words *gifted and talented* can be especially troublesome. Public school systems identify children as "gifted/talented" based on such criteria as consistently high grades, IQ levels, or exceptional ability in artistic areas, creative endeavors, or

> **You take people as far as they will go, not as far as you would like them to go.** [5]
>
> Jeannette Rankin,
> *American pacifist, suffragist, and congresswoman*

leadership. These criteria vary depending on the individual school district and the state in which it is located. Once children are identified, they are eligible for special services, such as enrichment activities and/or pull-out programs where specially trained teachers periodically remove students from their regular classrooms and teach them in another classroom with other similarly identified students. We must emphasize that when the term **gifts and talents** is used in this book, it refers to those special attributes that *your* child possesses, regardless of how others, including the public school system, have labeled or categorized your youngster.

Step 2:
Observe your child openly and
without judgment.

Look at your children and see them for who they really are. Sometimes parents are so busy guiding their child's choices, instilling appropriate values, and teaching proper behavior, that they fail to see the individual standing before them. Worse still, they often assume that their child is a mirror image of themselves, forgetting that children are separate and distinct individuals with their own likes and dislikes.

The following activity has worked successfully in helping parents begin to look at their children objectively. First, on a piece of paper, write down the labels or words usually used to describe your daughter or son. Next, take this piece of paper, rip it to shreds, and throw it in the trash. Finally, think carefully about your child and try to observe her or him in a fresh light, without preconceived notions. Imagine that you are an anthropologist doing fieldwork. Try to put aside prior perceptions and judgments. Watch without intruding as your child goes about his or her normal, everyday activities. Most important, look for those positive attributes that make your youngster unique.

There are two advantages to this approach. First, the information gathered is *relatively objective,* because what is observed reflects your child's behavior in a naturally occurring situation without manipulation or interference on your part. Second, the information gathered is *immediate,* because what you are observing is behavior that is occurring in the present, not behavior that occurred in the past or may occur in the future.

Obviously, it is impossible to discard all previous impressions and the solid base of knowledge you have accumulated over the years about your child. What is amazing, though, is how much farther along on the road to open observation and insight parents can travel by making such a small adjustment on their part.

Step 3:
Note only the positive about your child.

Assessing a child's weaknesses and areas of trouble is an extremely valid and important activity for educational purposes. However, for what you as a parent hope to accomplish through this book, it is suggested that you look only at the positive. Admittedly, this can be hard to do, especially for a child who has a remarkable knack for "pressing your buttons," or who manifests a significant number of negative traits in her or his behavioral repertoire. But once started, the process becomes easier and easier, followed by quite noteworthy benefits.

If you are having difficulty beginning this process, the following questions may help you get started. Say you are the parent of Carolyn, an only child, and you want to discover her particular areas of strength. You may ask yourself:

- Does Carolyn make friends easily?
- Does she seem interested in the larger social world, rather than just her immediate surroundings?
- Does she have stick-to-it-iveness when it comes to projects?
- Is she well organized?
- Does she have a passion for music or art?
- Is she good at solving problems she encounters?
- Does she have an unusually kind heart?
- Does she seem to especially enjoy physical activities?

- Does she feel comfortable talking in front of groups?
- Do peers tend to follow her lead?
- Does she love to build things?
- Does she seem most happy being outside?
- Does she think math is "fun"?
- Does she love to write?

There is no limit or order to the number of questions that can be asked. To get an accurate portrait of your child, devise a schedule that is convenient for you to make your observations. One possible schedule would be five- to ten-minute time periods, several times a day, over a two- to three-week period. In this way, extraneous variables, such as fatigue or illness on the part of you or your child, will not color your perception. It is also recommended that you observe your child in several different settings and situations. Always observing your son Carl at the dinner table, for instance, will give you less of a true picture of his abilities than if you observe him engaging in various activities, such as doing his homework, interacting with a neighbor, shopping with you at the grocery store, riding in the car on the way to school, or simply playing with his friends. Make a list of all the positive traits you observe. After you begin to feel comfortable with this procedure, it can become part of the way in which you parent—a parenting style, so to speak.

Step 4:
Identify your child's gifts
and talents.

By openly observing your child and asking yourself the necessary questions, you can begin not only to view your daughter or son in a positive and nurturing manner, but you can also start to *identify* her or his specific gifts and talents.

One effective way to identify your child's strengths is to take the list of positive traits you created in step 3 and cluster these traits into groupings of like characteristics. As an obvious example of traits that could be grouped together, notice the similar ring to the following descriptions of Jeremy, a feisty third grader: He loves to be outdoors, manifests a sensitive caring for all living things, is especially good with the family pet, and spends his free time reading about animals and writing poems with animal themes. This grouping suggests a boy whose compassion for and interest in animals is an especially strong area.

Or how about Jeremy's sister, Maria? She loves brain-teaser games, her favorite part of math at school is word problems, and she enjoys being in charge of the road map during long trips, especially figuring out how to get from point A to point B. Doesn't she sound like a youngster with good problem-solving skills?

You can also ask your child to identify her or his own strengths. Some children are quite forthright and savvy when it comes to assessing these areas. Karen may answer, "Oh, I'm better than most of my friends in reading," or "I make friends easily. I think everyone likes me."

Other children may be bewildered by the question, or perhaps they will be in a negative mood. With either of these scenarios, a parent is likely to hear "Oh, nothing," "I don't know," or maybe even "I'm good at being stupid." Not to worry. With the right line of questioning and a little help from you, children generally come around.

One approach is to ignore the negativity in the reply. A parental response of "That's silly, you're good at lots of things" or "Why are you saying that? You're so negative" can lead to a verbal power struggle or an unpleasant exchange. What you want to accomplish is to guide the youngster into a meaningful discussion about strengths. For example,

Roxanne may answer, "I'm not good at anything." Her dad can reply with a safe topic: "I've always thought of you as good at making things. Remember that great toy car you made for the neighborhood derby last year?" Perhaps Scott answers with an obviously silly remark: "Oh, I'm great at burping." His mom can shift into a different line of thought: "I hadn't thought of burping. Do you think you're better at throwing or catching?" Finding out what your child thinks of her or his own strengths can be illuminating and sometimes quite surprising.

Another suggestion for identifying your child's gifts and talents is to get an opinion from someone who knows your child well. You may even ask that person to observe your child for this purpose. Sometimes it takes another person to recognize traits that you as a parent simply don't see. A teacher, an older sibling, a family friend, a scout leader, or a grandparent can be a useful resource when it comes to learning more about your child. Parents may be reluctant to admit that someone else might know more about a particular aspect of their child than they do. In general, parents *are* the "experts" when it comes to knowing their daughters and sons, and they should trust their instincts. Once they've opened their minds and have attempted to get to know their children better, however, information from other sources becomes valid and welcome.

Sometimes this information comes in the form of the dreaded report card. Grades, ratings, and written evaluations from teachers are extremely important sources of data concerning your child. If Carolyn consistently gets Bs in everything except science, in which she always gets As, this is a fairly good indication that science is a strong area for her and probably one she enjoys, since children tend to like those subjects in which they excel.

Remember, though, that report cards do not reflect the whole being of your child. In fact, they generally represent only those traditional areas of functioning that our school systems tend to appreciate and reward, such as reading comprehension, mathematical skills, the ability to work independently and quietly, compliance with authority, and verbal skills (the latter, of course, only when requested).

Take the case of Carolyn, above. Adults might recognize her strength in science, but perhaps nobody has noticed that she spends recess playing with building blocks, loves to look at houses, store fronts, and office buildings on her way home from school, and when doodling, often draws neighborhoods that have libraries and civic centers. Carolyn may be a budding architect or urban planner, but her strengths and interests, although evident now, are not ones that are typically rewarded in the average school. It is important to look beyond the report card and realize that there is so much more to your child than what is reflected on that piece of paper.

Now let's look at some specific areas of strength. Do you recognize your child in any of the following chapters?

·2·

The Gift of Leadership

Let our children grow tall and
some taller than others if they
have it in them to do so. [6]

Margaret Thatcher,
former Prime Minister of Great Britain

What do we mean by leadership?

Leadership is one of those loaded terms that means different things to different people. For our purposes, however, leadership can be thought of as the ability to influence other people's actions or thoughts in a goal-directed manner. It's an intriguing and remarkable trait that some would even call mysterious. Most people would agree that leadership is a quality that is needed and valued, yet amazingly little is known about leadership in children. Although it is one of the categories used by some public school systems[7] to identify students as gifted/talented for placement in special programs, traditionally it is the one that has the fewest candidates. Why is a quality that is highly regarded also one about which little is known, and why are relatively few children with this trait identified as "gifted"?

One might argue that leadership is simply difficult to spot in children. This is untrue. Leadership is as easy to recognize in children as any other quality. The trick is to know what to look for.

Is your child a leader?

"Mom! Miguel is so-o-o bossy! He's always telling me what to do! Make him stop!" Does this sound familiar? Miguel is the type of child who is often perceived in a negative light by others. He is bossy, always telling his peers what to do, how to do it, and even *when* to do it. Ironically, Miguel may be manifesting his leadership qualities. The underlying communicative intent of his behavior may be quite positive. He wants to influence others. Unfortunately, Miguel hasn't yet learned how to do this in a positive, constructive manner.

Many youngsters like Miguel find their beginning efforts

unmercifully squashed by well-meaning adults as well as by irritated peers. We say "Miguel, stop bossing Chris around! Let her decide what she wants to play with."

Not only is the manner in which Miguel attempted to influence Chris being deliberately admonished, but the underlying intent of trying to influence others is being unintentionally punished. Instead of simply reprimanding him, what his parents need to do is to shape Miguel's behavior into a more socially acceptable manner. The problem lies in the fact that Miguel's leadership qualities are not being recognized by those around him. Rather, they are viewed as negative behaviors to be eliminated or at least diminished. Once parents learn to identify leadership qualities in their children, then they are much better prepared to help shape those qualities in socially appropriate and effective ways.

One way to start the process of recognizing leadership qualities is to look at the actions of your child without worrying about the consequences or the reactions of others. Here are examples of questions you may want to ask yourself:

- Does your child often tell other children what to do in play situations?
- Is your child quick to suggest family activities?
- Does she tell adults what to do?
- Does your child "correct" others when she thinks they are wrong?
- Does she purposefully show others what to do?
- Does your child indirectly show others what to do by example?
- Does she seem to enjoy being "the boss"?
- Does your child deliberately put herself at the head of the line or in the center of the circle during group activities?

- Does your child always have an opinion she insists on sharing?

The answers to questions such as these can help reveal a pattern of behaviors that reflects a potential leader.

There are different styles of leadership. Some people lead by the strength of their powerful personalities. A charismatic speaker such as Martin Luther King, Jr., would fall under this category. Others lead through the force of their ideas in a more quiet, reflective manner. Mahatma Gandhi would probably fall into this group. So you see, your child may be a leader of the future even though she or he doesn't appear to have a strong, extrovert-type personality. Moreover, even if your child does not appear to demonstrate particularly strong leadership qualities at this moment, these qualities may become visible when you shift gears and move on to the next level of observation.

Try examining the consequences and reactions of other people to your child. Here the emphasis is on observing not your child's behavior, but rather how people respond to your child. Let's say you are the parent of Miguel. Questions you can ask include:

- Do other children tend to "copy" what Miguel is doing?
- Do others often ask your child what he wants to do before they decide what they want to do?
- Do peers often clamor around him, want to stand next to him, be his partner, or dress like him?
- Do friends ask him for an opinion or advice?
- Is your child often picked by others as the leader of a group activity?
- Does the teacher treat him as a leader?

A person can be recognized as having leadership qualities not only by how she or he behaves, but also by the response of others to that behavior. Clearly, not all children will grow up to be leaders, which is perfectly fine. However, all children who demonstrate leadership qualities should be allowed to develop those qualities in a supportive and loving atmosphere. Many youngsters are "late bloomers." They may not manifest their strengths in this area until later on in life, perhaps when a particular opportunity or issue motivates them. Therefore, it is vitally important to help all children develop their leadership skills. Such skills are resources that are too precious to waste. Let's explore how you can encourage leadership in your child.

How can you develop your child's leadership skills?

One of the most effective ways to develop leadership skills is to talk about leadership with your child. Since leadership is difficult for adults to define, you can imagine how tough it is for children to put into words. By discussing the topic, the vocabulary and concepts surrounding leadership become a natural part of your child's world. Find out what your child thinks and knows before teaching her or him what *you* think and know. Listen to what your child has to say about the topic. You may be surprised and impressed by what you hear.

You can help children understand leadership by exposing them to examples of leadership. Begin by discussing leaders whom young people can relate to. For example, the Teenage Mutant Ninja Turtles or the Mighty Morphin Power Rangers will be much more meaningful to a child than Theodore Roosevelt. Likewise, the head of the PTA or the school principal will have more relevance than Gloria Steinem. Progressively, children can then be exposed to leaders who may be more removed from their immediate lives.

It is crucial to include males and females from different cultural backgrounds, of different ages, and from different fields of endeavor. Children need to realize that people can be leaders regardless of their sex, the country they come from, or the language they speak. Furthermore, they need to understand that leaders can be found in fields as diverse as politics, music, local community activities, and computer development. Once children grasp these ideas, they are truly on the road to seeing the endless possibilities inherent in leadership.

Did you know?
In 1981 Sandra Day O'Connor was the first woman to be appointed to the Supreme Court. In 1967 Thurgood Marshall was the first African American to be appointed. Roger B. Taney was the first Roman Catholic, appointed in 1836. Louis D. Brandeis was the first Jewish justice, appointed in 1916.

Literature is a terrific way for parents to expose children to leaders. Through books, newspapers, and magazines you can have a dialogue with your child concerning the qualities that make a leader. See if your child can identify if the person is/was a good speaker or a positive thinker. Relevant materials can be found in the most unlikely places. Fairy tales, classics, poetry, interviews with popular entertainers, and even human interest stories in the sports section of your local newspaper may tap into leadership. A listing of relevant books can be found at the end of this chapter. Such reading materials make wonderful gifts, bedtime reading, subjects for dinner discussions, and additions to your child's school library. Remember that all these books do not have to be purchased. Many can be found in your local public library. The books can even be shared among the children in your car pool or the neighborhood youngsters.

Most children love movies, and renting videos seems to have become an increasingly popular pastime. Here we find another accessible means of exploring the lives of various leaders. At the end of this chapter you will find a compilation of appropriate movies on video you may want to check out. Children learn best from movies when they have been given bits of information or things to look for beforehand. For example, if the movie deals with the life of a famous painter who changed the course of art, why not show your child one of the painter's most famous works from an art book before viewing the film? Likewise, you may want to discuss the specific contribution the painter made to the art world. How about an amusing anecdote from her or his life? If the painter worked with watercolors, why not let your child dabble in watercolors before seeing the movie? These "presets" increase a child's interest and motivation, and they also help direct your child's attention to the subject matter. In addition, learning new material is facilitated when it can

Suggested Activities
That Foster Leadership

- On the way to school, during the car pool, **pick one child to be the leader of the day**. This child would be the one to assign seating to the other children, choose which radio station or cassette tape to listen to, or select what word game to play.

- That good old traditional game **follow the leader is a favorite for encouraging leadership.** In case you've forgotten the rules, the players stand in a circle, with the leader in the middle. The players follow the actions of the leader. In other words, they must do whatever the leader does. After a preset amount of time (for example, two minutes), a new leader is chosen by the person in the center, and the players then follow the new leader.

- When your child has friends over, suggest they put on a play. **Let each child take a turn being the director or the star** of the play. You can even provide a special director's chair or "star seat." It always helps to have a special box or bag of dress-up clothes available. Goodies that can be collected for later use are old Halloween costumes, inexpensive costume jewelry, used clothes that are no longer wearable, and fun accessories (such as clunky boots, oversized hats, or colorful scarves).

- Leaders have a good feeling about themselves, leading to self-confidence and the willingness to take risks in life. **Acknowledge your child's efforts.** Concentrate on the positive. Be your child's biggest fan.

- **Have your child interview a member of the school board or community** about her or his position of leadership. You may need to provide some help with setting up the appointment and coming up with appropriate questions, but it is best to give guidance and assistance only when necessary.

- **Reinforce creative efforts.** Leaders are able to pull together different elements and come up with a new thought or plan of action. For example, praise those times when your child comes up with a new way of doing something, such as bathing the dog in a new, goofy way, no matter how silly it may seem to you as an adult. This doesn't mean you have to let your child put Fido in a wagon and leave him out in the pouring rain (!). It does mean that you can playfully help your child figure out why a certain plan is not workable, while at the same time acknowledging that your youngster has come up with a new way of doing things. (See Chapter Four for more on this topic.)

- **Children should have abundant opportunities to visualize, or imagine, themselves as leaders,** so that the possibility of being a leader becomes a part of who they are. So the next time you are playing the "Pretend you're..." game, try suggesting positions of leadership for your child to role-play. For example, if you're stuck in traffic and you need a quick word game to pass the time, try: "Hey, Adam. Pretend you're the president of General Motors. That's the huge company that made this car. Can you think of something you would add to this kind of car that would help people when they get stuck in traffic jams?" Children never seem to tire of pretending. (Too bad so many adults have lost this marvelous and joyful ability.) Try switching places and letting your child give you a "pretend" scenario to play out. You'll be amazed at how much fun it can be.

- Imagination is a powerful tool. **Ask your child what our country would be like if it had no leader.** You can substitute "school," "city," an organization, or any number of things for "country." Through such dialogue, the necessity of leadership will become clearer.

- **Encourage debate in your home.** Leaders need to have excellent verbal skills to accomplish their goals. They need to articulate their ideas to others in a clear and organized manner; they must be comfortable speaking to others; and they need to be able to persuade and inspire those they are leading. The more children are allowed to practice these skills, the better.

- **Help your child organize a home, community, or school improvement project.** Recruiting siblings and friends, deciding on the objective of the project, coming up with a workable plan, and carrying it out successfully are all aspects that encourage leadership.

be attached to preexisting, and already learned information.

Another way to encourage leadership in your child is to let your child "practice" being a leader. The more opportunities young people are given to try out leadership skills, the more effective they will be in influencing others in a positive manner.

Although this last suggestion will be discussed in more detail in Chapter Four, it does raise an interesting question: What underlying skills must a person have to be able to accomplish the higher level skill of leadership? It is not enough to encourage leadership; children also need practice in developing the components of leadership. Below is a list of such subskills. You can probably think of others.

- looking at a problem situation and focusing on a specific objective
- moving from a specific objective to a workable plan of action
- delegating tasks among group members
- realizing how to share leadership
- knowing how to recognize what you know and can do
- recognizing what you do not know and cannot do
- knowing how to use resources to find out what you don't know
- recognizing the strengths and weaknesses of the group members
- being effective at conflict resolution
- realizing how and when to modify procedures or style when necessary
- being able to listen and communicate well
- knowing how to handle dissent or disagreement
- helping keep group members focused on the task
- knowing how to disseminate information

- being able to rise above the ordinary and formulate a vision that inspires others
- knowing how to evaluate progress
- being a creative thinker

Whew! It's amazing how complex the role of leader can be. It becomes even more complicated, however, when the moral and ethical responsibility underlying leadership is considered. Children absolutely love talking about this topic. They almost seem to have an innate desire to ponder the "right or wrong" aspect of an issue—or any issue, for that matter. You are guaranteed a spirited dialogue if you pose the following question to your youngster: "Is leadership always used for good purposes, or can it be used for bad purposes?" Allow the topic to be shaped by what your child has to say.

Depending on your child's maturation level, mood, and interests, the conversation may take off in any of a number of directions. Perhaps the topic of "bad leaders/good leaders" may be pursued. Maybe the dialogue will center around the question "Do leaders have a special responsibility to use their power in a positive and moral way?" Whatever avenue it takes is fine. The point is that you want your child to start thinking and talking about these issues. At the same time, you want to find out what your child knows and how your child feels about this topic.

When talking to your child, remember that children are a heterogeneous group. In other words, there are many differences among them. There may be two siblings, Jennifer and Paul, who are both extremely bright. Jennifer may get very excited about the topic and go on and on about why a leader should be a good person. She may have so much to say on the subject that you may wish you had never brought it up! Paul, however, may seem only vaguely interested. At his first opportunity he may start talking about something completely different. Both scenarios are quite natural.

It's best not to push or force a topic. By paying attention to verbal, paraverbal, and nonverbal cues given by your child, you can usually tell when to continue or discontinue a conversational topic. Verbal cues pertain to *what* a child says ("I've got a great idea"). Paraverbal cues refer to *how* a child says something ("I don't really care" said in a whining, high-pitched tone). Nonverbal cues are associated with body language (shrugging the shoulders, frowning, rolling the eyes, and so forth). If a topic needs to be discontinued, it can always be brought up again at a later date.

You might also want to pair your child with a leader. This type of mentor relationship is an effective way for your child to get hands-on experience and see leadership in action. Do you have a friend who holds a position of leadership at her job? Do you know a community member who could shed some light on the activities of a leader? Does your child have a friend who is a leader in scouts, school, church/temple activities, sports, or community service organizations? The best mentors are those who are willing to encourage, guide, and support your child. They should be willing to have an ongoing relationship that will help your youngster develop the skills and self-confidence necessary for a leadership role. However, don't overlook those people who may have a more transitory place in your child's life. Part-time mentorships are better than none at all. The possibilities are endless.

One readily accessible way to foster leadership is to encourage your child's involvement in extracurricular activities. A ten-year study conducted with more than five hundred high school student leaders revealed that almost two thirds were involved in out-of-school clubs, organizations, and athletics, while more than half participated in fine arts activities.[8] These results suggest that involvement in extracurricular activities is highly correlated with leadership in school. Furthermore, leadership in extracurricular activities, rather than academic achievement, has been found to be more highly correlated with adult leadership.[9] Even if your child isn't an above-average student, extracurricular activities may be a positive influence paving the way for a leadership role as an adult. Why wait until high school? Why not help your youngster find an outside interest during the elementary years?

> **Children do not have to wait to be leaders.**

Here are some final related topics pertaining to leadership that you can discuss with your child:

- the difference between power and leadership
  (Who decides? Which is better?)
- it's OK to be a follower
  (You can't have leaders without followers.)
- the difference between "blindly" following someone and following intelligently
  (questioning leaders)
- the personal benefits of being a leader
  (feelings of accomplishment and fulfillment)
- how children can manifest their leadership
  (as mentioned before: scouts, school, church/temple activities, sports, community service organizations)
- why leaders in one field don't always make good role models in another area
  (Different qualities may be needed for different endeavors.)
- the media's influence in creating leaders
  (the power of selective reporting, sound bites, and physical attributes)

Leadership is a precious quality that needs to be encouraged and nurtured in our youth. Leaders not only spur us to action, they inspire us, they motivate us, and they enrich our lives.

A Conversation About Leadership

One way to better understand leadership is to talk to someone who holds a position of leadership. Below is a conversation with **Linda Havard,** vice president of corporate planning, Atlantic Richfield Company. She is also immediate past president of an organization called Leadership California. You will find her thoughts and perceptions enlightening.

Q: *Linda, could you describe your organization and its objectives?*

A: Leadership California is a nonprofit leadership development program for women in California. Our purpose is to bring together a mosaic of women from all different segments of California, for example: different cultures, different occupations, and different ages. We help them to deal with the many issues facing the state, and then ask them to go back to their communities and professions and work to make California a better place.

Q: *How would you define leadership?*

A: Leadership is almost an aura; it's something inside of you that causes people to want to follow you. It's really indescribable, a combination of elements, actually. Inspiration.

Q: *What skills do you think are necessary for a person to be an effective leader?*

A: Reflection, exploration, somebody who can think of alternatives, somebody who can listen, who can cut through the morass and see the central issue, one who can see the relationship between disparate ideas.

Q: *Do you remember at what age you started to demonstrate leadership qualities? What were they?*

A: When I was about ten years old, I remember being the leader of a softball team. I was a good shortstop, and I had to analyze what role I would best serve for the team. I had to think about my value along with that of the other team members. Around the same time, I also remember having to evaluate my strengths when it came to schoolwork. I was very good at math and spelling but decided to put my energies into math. I didn't even enter the spelling bee. I chose where I would put my efforts. I guess you could call it the opposite of self-aggrandizement. The quality of self-evaluation is important for leadership.

Q: *How has being a leader enriched your life?*

A: Well, at first it scared me. I didn't set out to be a leader. I turned around and people were following me. I've tried to pass on what I've learned to women so they can experience what I have experienced. My life is fulfilling because I have been able to rethink my priorities and choose what I want to give back to others.

Q: *What suggestions would you have for parents who wish to encourage the development of leadership in their children?*

A: I would suggest that parents encourage the little instances of reflection, the little examples of leadership. I would also suggest building up self-esteem and having a positive attitude. Don't expect too much. Your children will continue to grow. Each piece adds up to something. Finally, don't lay expectations on your children of the type of leader you want them to be. Let them be who they are.

Where to Go for More Information on Leadership

There are many resources to be tapped if you would like to know more about developing leadership in children. Here are some examples:

- the teachers and other staff at your child's school
- the coordinator of gifted/talented programs in your school district
- the Gifted and Talented Coordinator for the Department of Education in your state (Contact your state's Department of Education.)
- local, state, and national conferences on education
- local parent support groups, which often provide enrichment programs (If they don't have a program on leadership development, why not help them start one?)
- journals on child development, parenting, and education, which can be found at your local library:
  Child Development
  Exceptional Children
  Journal for the Education of Gifted Children
  Roeper Review
  Young Children

- local, state, and national organizations, such as the following:

American Red Cross—Youth Associate

(encourages volunteerism, leadership development, community involvement)

> Program and Services Department
> 431 18th St., NW
> Washington, DC 20006
> (202) 639-3039

The Association for the Gifted (TAG)

(major clearinghouse for information on gifted education, including leadership development)

> Council for Exceptional Children
> 1920 Association Dr.
> Reston, VA 22091-1589
> (800) 8456-CEC

The National Research Center on the Gifted & Talented

(collects and disseminates research on gifted and talented education, including leadership development)

> The University of Connecticut
> 362 Fairfield Rd., U-7
> Storrs, CT 06269-2007

One to One

(develops mentoring programs between people in business and students)

> 2801 M St., NW
> Washington, DC 20007
> (202) 338-3844

- books on leadership in children:
  Roets, L. F. (1992). *Leadership: A Skills Training Program*. Des Moines: Leadership Publishers, Inc. This is a book filled with classroom activities and geared for teachers, but as a parent, you'll find some clever ideas you might like to try.

  Sisk, D. A. & D. J. Shallcross (1986). *Leadership: Making Things Happen*. Buffalo, N.Y.: Bearly Limited. More sound ideas for developing leadership.

Books With Leadership Themes

Billings, M. S. & H. (1993 & 1994). *Winners*. Austin, Texas: Steck-Vaughn Co. (800) 531-5015. Series of low-reading-level (grades 2–4) and high-interest (grades 5–12) stories of Nobel Prize winners, Hall of Fame honorees, Presidential Medal of Freedom recipients, entertainers, and so forth.

d'Aulaire, I. & E. P. (1957). *Abraham Lincoln*. New York: Bantam Doubleday Dell Publishing Group (grades 3–6). Caldecott Medal winner. Dell Picture Yearling Special.

DiSomma, E. V. & M. L. McTiernan. Illustrated by A. Jones (1987). J. F. Cooper, *The Last of the Mohicans*. Dormac, Inc. Available through Redmond, Wash.: Edmark (reading level 4.0). (800) 362-2890. Simple English Classics Series. Explores leadership qualities.

Falstein, M. (1994). *Freedom Fighters*. Paramus: Globe Fearon. (800) 848-9500. Five biographies of leaders in the fight for equality: Nelson Mandela, Fannie Lou Hamer, Cesar Chavez, Malcolm X, and Martin Luther King, Jr. (reading level 3.5–4.0; interest level 5–12).

Freedman, R. (1987). *Lincoln: A Photobiography*. New York: Clarion Books (meant for grades 6–8, but is appropriate for younger children if emphasis is placed on the photographs). Beautiful biography of Lincoln with fascinating photographs. Newbery Medal winner.

Gleiter, J. & K. Thompson (1985). *Great Tales: Annie Oakley*. Nashville: Ideals Publishing Corp. (grades 3–6). Leadership qualities.

Karnes, F. A. & S. M. Bean (1993). *Girls & Young Women Leading the Way: 20 True Stories About Leadership*. Minneapolis: Free Spirit Publishing (grades 3–6). (800) 735-7323. Inspirational true stories with practical tips.

Krensky, S. Illustrated by N. Green. (1991). *Christopher Columbus*. STEP into Reading series, Step 2 book. New York: Random House (grades 1–3).

McGuire, J. V. (1992). *No Negatives: A Guide to Leadership for Young People*. College Custom Series. New York: McGraw-Hill (grades 4 and up). Helpful hints for children, from time management to self-esteem.

McLeish, V. & K. Illustrated by D. Burnard & A. Snell (1991). *Troll Famous People*. USA: Troll Associates/HarperCollins (grades 3-6). Short biographies, including a chapter on leaders (Alexander the Great, Cleopatra, Ayatollah Khomeini, Sun Yat-Sen).

Rodriguez, C. (1991). *Cesar Chavez*. New York: Chelsea House (grades 3–6). Hispanics of Achievement Series. Biography.

Seuss, Dr. (1950). *Yertle the Turtle and Other Stories*. New York: Random House. Geared toward younger children, but even elementary-age children love this tale of one who abuses power.

Films and Videos With Leadership Themes

Animal Farm (1955). Animated version based on George Orwell's satire. Explores a struggle for leadership and leadership gone wrong. Halas & Batchelor, U.K. 72 min.

Apache: Geronimo on the Warpath (1993). Documentary video. Time Warner Viewer's Edge. 90 min.

Boys Town (1938). Spencer Tracy won a Best Actor Academy Award for his role as a priest who founds a home for wayward boys. MGM/UA Home Video. 94 min.

Christopher Columbus: The Discovery (1992). 120 min.

Cool Runnings. (1993). Reluctant leadership. Disney. 100 min.

Dave (1993). Explores leadership qualities and use/abuse of leadership. Warner/Northern Lights. 110 min.

Geronimo (1962). United Artists. 101 min.

Hook (1992). Continuation of Peter Pan legend; explores the idea of questioning leadership. Tri-Star/Amblin. 144 min.

Land Before Time, The (1988). A young dinosaur leads a band of little dinosaurs. Amblin. 66 min.

League of Their Own, A (1992). Leadership of a women's baseball team in an unlikely guise; the need for leadership. Parkway/Columbia. 128 min.

Men in Space (1989). 20th anniversary celebration of *Apollo XI*'s historic 1969 moon landing. 45 min.

Mighty Ducks, The (1992). The need for teamwork and leadership. Disney. 101 min.

Oliver! (1968). Leadership used for good and bad purposes. Columbia/Romulus. 146 min.

Peter Pan (1953). Animated. Disney. 76 min.

Story of Henry Ford, The (1991). Time Warner Viewer's Edge. 55 min.

Tucker: The Man and His Dream (1988). Determined leadership and leadership qualities. Lucasfilm/Zoetrope. 111 min.

Wizard of Oz, The (1939). Dorothy as leader. MGM. 100 min.

Young Mr. Lincoln (1939). The early years of Abraham Lincoln. 20th Century Fox/Cosmopolitan. 101 min.

Young Winston (1972). The early years of Winston Churchill. Columbia/Open Road. 157 min.

·3·

The Gift of Creativity

These are the days of miracles
and wonder, so don't cry,
baby, don't cry. [10]

Paul Simon,
American songwriter

What is creativity?

C reativity is one of the most exciting but least understood gifts your child can possess. Is it a trait a person either has or doesn't have? Can it be fostered? Does it always manifest itself in the arts? Do we all have a potential for creativity? Is there a universal definition of creativity? Let's examine this enigmatic characteristic.

Creativity plays an important role in all areas of life. It can be found in everyday settings and in all areas of human endeavor. Traditionally, it has been associated with the worlds of art, dance, drama, literature, interior design, urban planning, and architecture. In reality, creativity is also necessary in areas such as science, business, law, medicine, engineering, leadership, and even parenting!

There are hundreds of definitions and scores of models used to explain creativity. One of the simplest ways to look at this particular characteristic is to think of it as the ability to act on ideas, facts, and materials in new, unusual, or unique ways. This explains only one aspect, however. Creativity is really multidimensional, so it is best to think of it as an umbrella term used to describe a combination of characteristics. One way to get a clearer understanding of these characteristics is to examine creative individuals and note what sets them apart from less creative people.

Creative individuals are believed to use certain thinking abilities more than those who are less creative. Some creative people are stronger in some of these abilities than others. Although not exhaustive, these key properties can be grouped into four main categories: **fluency, flexibility, originality,** and **elaboration.**[11] An examination of each of these thinking competencies will clarify what creativity is all about.

Fluency refers to the ability to generate a flow of ideas, consequences, or solutions to a problem. A child who demonstrates fluency reaches beyond one or two possibilities. The quantity, as well as quality, of responses is important. Fluency increases as a child becomes more able to generate a greater quantity of responses at will.

Flexibility is the ability to use many different approaches or strategies in solving a problem. An individual who is flexible is willing to change direction and modify an approach without becoming flustered or being thrown off course. She or he is not a rigid thinker but a fluid thinker. Flexibility increases as it becomes easier for a child to adapt to new information and situations.

Originality is the ability to produce unusual, different, and unique responses to a problem. A child who manifests originality thinks of the unlikely, the unexpected, the fresh. This is the characteristic that most people associate with creativity. Children develop their originality when they are allowed to be playful and spontaneous.

Finally, **elaboration** is the ability to develop or expand one's ideas, stories, or illustrations. People who elaborate broaden the original concept; they take it further. For example, a young girl elaborates when after being asked to draw a house, she also draws the neighborhood surrounding the house. Elaboration is increased when children show a commitment to the completion of a project or the solution of a problem, and when they are given the opportunity to expand on that project or problem.

By examining these four abilities, several things become apparent: (1) a person must interact with the environment in some way in order to create the opportunity for creative thought or action; (2) each of these abilities can be encouraged and developed; (3) all people are capable of such action and thought to some degree, depending on their developmental level; and (4) a child can be strong in certain specific ability areas of creativity while being weak in others.

Is your child creative?

All individuals are capable of creative thought and action. Even children who are mentally retarded[12] and those with learning disabilities[13] demonstrate creative thinking. It is not an ability that is reserved for a select few.

In general, there is a positive relationship between intelligence and creativity. Most highly creative persons are also above average in intelligence, although high intellectual functioning doesn't necessarily insure that a person will also be highly creative.[14] Therefore, the higher your child's intelligence, the more likely she or he is to manifest creative thought and action, but keep in mind that your child has the potential for creative thought and action no matter what intellectual ability level she or he is functioning at. There is even evidence to suggest that creativity is more dependent on emotional and personality factors than intellectual variables.[15] For example, how does your child respond to difficult situations? What types of behavioral patterns or styles are manifested? Does your youngster have the courage to try something different?

Other documentation shows that many people who are highly creative as adults did not receive exceptionally high grades in school.[16] There is no clear, positive connection between academic achievement in youth and creative ability in adulthood, probably because academic achievement is based far more on convergent thinking than on divergent thinking. In other words, how well a student does in school depends more on "getting the right answers" than being a creative thinker. To reiterate the discussion in Chapter One concerning report cards, grades in school reflect only one aspect of your child's functioning, that is, performance in school. Your daughter or son is much more than what is represented by a report card.

Research has also identified a cluster of behaviors that is indicative of creative thought and action. If you'd like to discover, for example, whether your son is particularly creative, here are some questions, many adapted from Kirschenbaum's Creative Behavior Inventory,[17] that you may find useful:

- Does he tell stories with a verbal flourish?
- Does he think of multiple solutions to a problem?
- Is he opinionated?
- Does he usually ask lots of questions?
- Does he add a personal touch to his projects and creations?
- Does he like to talk about complex subjects?
- Does he question the status quo and authority figures?
- Does he have an appetite for learning?
- Is he self-confident?
- Does he enjoy exploring new ideas?
- Does he have a playful attitude toward solving problems, using make-believe, humor, and so forth?
- Does he notice details yet see "the big picture"?
- Does he tend to intensify his efforts when faced with an obstacle or mistake?
- Does he seek adventure?
- Does he dislike conformity?

The above questions will help direct you toward your child's creative ability. Every youngster has the potential for creative thought and action. You, as the parent, have a tremendous opportunity and responsibility to help your daughter or son develop her or his creative abilities.

Creativity Training Programs

M any short-term and long-term creativity training programs have been developed in education, industry, and business. Some have been more effective than others. Those that have been most successful in developing creative thought and action are the ones that include a wide-ranging program using a variety of materials, and that foster affective and personality, as well as cognitive, or intellectual, variables.[18] According to these findings, if you want your child to learn to approach real-life problems in a creative fashion, you should encourage emotional and attitudinal changes, as well as teach specific intellectual strategies. You will also need to give your child opportunities to deal with real-life dilemmas, using many different materials and situations.

How to help your child develop creativity.

Let's take a look at Crystal. She's a third grader who has been given an assignment to write a poem about wolves for her science class. That night at home, Crystal decides to cut out her paper in the shape of a wolf's head before she writes her poem on it. In one scenario, Crystal's mom mumbles, "Honey, that's a good idea, but you just don't have time. Hurry up. It's almost bedtime. Write your poem and let's get going." In another scenario, Crystal's mom knows it is getting late but realizes it's no big deal if bedtime is put off another five minutes. She replies, "Honey, that's a great idea." The next day at school, Crystal's teacher likes the poem and its presentation so much that she hangs it up on the bulletin board for all to see. The teacher decides that for the next written assignment she is going to ask all the children in the class to present their poems in the same way.

In the first case, Crystal's mom, although well meaning, has squelched her daughter's attempt to be creative. In the latter case, however, creativity has been encouraged. Crystal's mom gave her daughter both the *time* and the *encouragement* she needed to express herself creatively. One of the most effective ways to nurture creative abilities in your child is to provide the extra needed time to elaborate and be fluent, flexible, and original. It is practically impossible for a child to be creative without being given the time to analyze situations, explore options, imagine new possibilities, and evaluate his or her progress. Give your child that extra fifteen minutes here or an hour there. It is often difficult to do, given our fast-paced modern world, but the rewards will be well worth the effort.

Another way to encourage creativity is to nurture divergent thinking. Much of what children are expected to learn depends on what is called convergent thinking. This type of thinking refers to those situations where one is supposed to come up with a correct answer or solution after being given the necessary information. *What is 2 x 2?* is an example of a question that requires convergent thinking. There is a conventional, correct answer.

On the one hand, divergent thinking, first introduced as "divergent production" by Guilford in 1968,[19] also represents the process of coming up with information from given information. It differs, though, because the emphasis is on the quantity and variety of responses. An open-ended question is asked, and any number of responses is generated. *What are all the uses you can think of for an empty birdhouse?* is an example of a question that requires divergent thinking.

Data exist[20] which suggest that initial solutions to a given problem tend to be the more conventional responses, while the greater the number of solutions generated, the higher the likelihood of producing an original response. This is an exciting finding. It means that the more answers your child is allowed to come up with, the higher the probability

Questions to Encourage Divergent Thinking (adapted from Arnold[21])

+ Can you think of anything else?

+ What if you had magical powers and you could do anything?

+ What else could be done?

+ Could you change it in some way?

+ What happens if you do the opposite?

+ What could you do if you wanted to be *really* silly?

+ Could you use it in another way?

+ Can you add more color, sound, time, space, strength?

+ What would happen if (i.e. you had all the money you needed)?

+ Is there another way to do it?

she or he will demonstrate creative responses. You need to provide opportunities for your child to brainstorm, to generate ideas, possibilities, and solutions. Use probing questions and allow your youngster to *exhaust* the possibilities. No idea should be criticized, and the more "way out" the idea, the better.

Although this type of thinking is not synonymous with creativity, divergent thinking tests are probably the most commonly used measurement of children's potential for creative thought.[22]

Such tests appear to reflect a person's creative potential. Yet how creatively a person functions in life is based on much more than potential; opportunities, situational variables, motivational factors, emotional and personality characteristics, health, and parental creativity also come into play. Therefore, another way for you to develop your child's creativity is to provide a home environment in which creativity is prized. Because children face enormous social pressures to conform, it is important to praise novel solutions to problems. Reward imaginative behavior. Give your child room to be different, and try not to be self-conscious yourself.

Most important, examine your own attitude toward failure. Young people will not try for the unconventional, the new perspective, if they feel unsafe doing so. Failure is inherent in an atmosphere of open inquiry. Mistakes are a natural part of life, and failure is an effective tool for learning. You will be fostering creativity if your attitudes are conducive to "reaching for the stars."

Another way to encourage creativity is to provide your child with problems and encourage creative solutions. One possibility is to present silly problems that foster the imagination, such as: "Uh-oh, what would happen if *all* the grocery stores closed down for a month? What would we do for food?"

You could also put forth more realistic, less fanciful dilemmas, such as: "What are we going to do? You're supposed to be at soccer practice at 5:00, Cathy needs to be picked up at school at 4:45, and I need to be home by 5:00 for the delivery of the new washing machine. We can't do it all. Do you have any suggestions?"

Praise the ideas that are generated. If some are unworkable, help your child come up with reasons why the suggestions would not be feasible. You can reinforce the effort while simultaneously helping your youngster evaluate her or his ideas. Reinforcement is a complex phenomenon. Reinforcement that is functionally connected to the targeted behavior is far more effective than reinforcement that is not. If possible, carry out the suggestion, making it clear that your child's idea "saved the day." This is more likely to increase the probability of creative thought in the future than merely using praise alone. Try it next time when confronted with an appropriate situation. There's no greater reward for your child than having her or his suggestion followed.

A further caution concerning reinforcement has to do with the difference between praise and encouragement. More and more childhood specialists are cautioning against the overuse of praise, suggesting instead an increase in the use of encouragement. In one review of the literature,[23] it is pointed out that praise ("You're such a good boy!" or "I love the necklace you made!") can actually have negative effects on children. It can give the impression that parental love and acceptance are dependent on good behavior or the successful completion of a task. It can also discourage children from attempting difficult tasks because they fear that praise will be withheld from them if they don't succeed.

Parents can think in terms of encouraging the process as opposed to praising the final product. For instance, instead of the general statement "You're such a good boy!" a parent could make note of a specific element of the behavior: "I notice you're getting your homework done before turning on the television." Rather than "I love the necklace you made!" a parent may comment, "The alternating of the blue and red beads makes a beautiful pattern." Listen to the words you use to reinforce your child. See if you can decrease the praise and increase the encouragement.

An additional, significant way to foster creativity in your youngster is to encourage the exploration of the arts. Art, music, language arts, drama, and dance are not only enjoyable leisure activities in and of themselves, they are a marvelous way to express and evaluate personal feelings, solve problems, and generate and communicate ideas. Furthermore, they provide opportunities to develop the thinking abilities of fluency, flexibility, originality, and elaboration, which we discussed earlier.

Suggested Art Activities That Help to Foster Creative Thinking Skills

- Have your child draw a scene using pencil and paper. The more complex the scene, the better. Then **ask her or him to tell you all the colors she or he would use in that picture.**

- Suggest your youngster think of a particular emotion. **Ask her or him to make up a dance that expresses that emotion.** See if you can guess which emotion is being portrayed. (This is a great activity to do if your child has friends over.) Then, give your child an emotion to portray and have her or him come up with different types of movement exercises to represent that emotion.

- If you have a family pet, **ask your child to think of *all* the possible nicknames** for that pet. Then suggest your youngster write a poem using those nicknames.

- **Give your daughter or son a hodgepodge of art materials** (such as yarn, glue, pieces of wood, colored pens, cotton balls, old magazines, scraps of fabric, string, tape, and glitter). Don't give any instructions. See what happens.

- **Find a spot in the house where you "need" some artwork** (the refrigerator, a wall, a nightstand, even the back of your checkbook!). Ask your child to come up with something. Provide guidelines and materials only if needed.

- **Have your daughter or son compose a "Good morning" song.** Record it on a tape recorder and play the song each morning during breakfast. After a few days, ask your child to make it longer, shorter, faster, sillier, whatever. Rerecord and play the new version.

- If your child collects something of interest (baseball cards, buttons, dolls, unicorns, stamps, and so forth), **suggest she or he design an appropriate container to store and display the collection.**

- Remember that box of miscellaneous photographs that's collecting dust in the closet? You know, the duplicates, the fuzzy shots, and the ones you just don't have room for in your photo albums. Give the box to your budding creative thinker and **ask that the photographs be categorized or organized in some manner.** Provide four or six brightly colored large envelopes and a marking pen. Halfway through the project give your youngster some additional materials, perhaps scissors, crayons, and several smaller envelopes. If necessary, help your child be flexible and integrate the new materials into the project.

- Is it Dad's birthday? As a present, **suggest that your child put on a skit** to represent some particular characteristic of Dad. Have your video camera ready; you'll want to save this for posterity.

- One way to reinforce creative thought, while teaching the main components of story writing at the same time, is by **playing the "short story game."** You and your child are the players. One person comes up with a character, a problem or conflict, and some type of complication that will make it hard for the character to solve the problem. Example:

Daniel is a ten-year-old with dark curly hair and a big grin. He's very funny. In fact, his friends call him "Clown." One day Daniel oversleeps and wakes up an hour after school has begun. His mom has already left for work, and his older brother, who was supposed to wake him, has also overslept. To make matters worse, this is the day that Daniel is supposed to give his oral report on dinosaurs to the class. He races down the street to school. As he's approaching the front door he realizes he forgot to get dressed! He is still wearing his PJs.

Each player comes up with a solution and shares it with the other player verbally, in writing, or on tape. Now it's the other player's turn. He or she changes one of the components of the story. The same character and conflict can be used, but a different complication is proposed. Again, both players create and share solutions. Children love this activity, and it "shakes up" their imagination in a fun manner.

◆ Give your youngster a paper with a squiggly line on it. **Ask your daughter or son to draw an object out of that squiggly line and then tell you a story about it.** This is especially enjoyable if you have a group of children participating. One child may make an animal out of the line; another may draw a spaceship. It's fun to see the many results that come from one simple line.

At the age of twenty-nine, the great author Kafka suddenly discovered that he was a writer. He recorded this moment of insight in his diary in September 1912:

> This story, "The Judgement," I wrote at one sitting during the night of 22nd–23rd, from ten o'clock at night to six o'clock in the morning. I was hardly able to pull my legs out from under the desk, they had got so stiff from sitting. The fearful strain and joy, how the story developed before me, as if I were advancing over water…How everything can be said, how, for everything, for the strangest fancies there awaits a great fire in which they perish and rise up again…Only in this way can writing be done, only with such coherence, with such a complete opening out of the body and soul.[24]

Although there are recorded instances, such as the above, in which creative thought and effort seem to pour forth easily from a person during a magical moment, most creative production takes hard work. Modifications, revisions, and sometimes even discarding the initial effort and starting over from scratch are not uncommon. You can help develop your child's creativity by acknowledging the effort that is often required in creative action and thought. Point out how often you've had to edit your last report for work. Show the changes you made to the dining room centerpiece before you were finally satisfied with it. Children need to learn that products of value, especially creative ones, take time and effort.

> **Every generation must go further than the last or what's the use in it? A baker's son must bake better bread—a miner's son—each generation a mite further.** [25]
>
> Wilhelmina Kemp Johnstone,
> *Bahamian poet and writer*

Another suggestion for fostering creativity is to help your child become computer literate. The use of computers, especially hypermedia, in which text and images are electronically integrated and accessed, is particularly conducive to creative thought and action.[26] There is evidence that students who make use of such technology are more curious, more assertive, more willing to tackle challenging topics,[27] more motivated, and willing to spend greater amounts of time on their projects[28] than are students without access to such equipment. Children need to experiment and play around with different ways of expressing their ideas. Solving problems by preparing databases of information, such as combining text, images, and sound, using scanners, and accessing information from around the world, is a perfect avenue for such exploration.

I've discovered that my child is creative. Now what?

What should you do if you've ascertained that your daughter, Kristin, is especially creative? Talk to her and her teacher about your observations. Ask that your daughter be assessed for eligibility for special gifted and talented programs in her school district. A meeting will be arranged with you, Kristin, her teacher, the special education teacher, and probably an administrator from the school. Bring appropriate documentation from home, such as projects, artwork, teachers' comments, test scores, and impressions from appropriate community members. Be an advocate for your child.

If it turns out that Kristin is not eligible for the gifted and talented program in her school district, there is no cause for dismay. This does not mean she is low in creativity. It simply means that the school system did not find that she met the preestablished criteria for inclusion in their program. Perhaps the assessment measures that were used did not take into account the particular creative thinking abilities that are Kristin's strong points.

Did you know?
We are born with more than 100 billion neural cells in the brain, ready to be used. [29]

If you feel that the assessment was not conducted properly or did not measure the appropriate areas of ability, speak to your child's teacher or contact the representative for gifted and talented education in the school district. Request another assessment. Regardless of the eventual outcome, you should continue to provide opportunities at home for creative thought and action. Persist in encouraging creative endeavors in those areas where Kristin shows an interest. Your daughter will continue to grow creatively and be happier for it.

Creativity is somewhat like bringing order out of chaos; it is not creating chaos out of order. A note about how to keep your parental sanity while fostering your child's creativity may be in order! At times, too much freedom can cause problems. Some young people easily lose control when behavioral and situational limits are not placed on them. Children should not be allowed to be destructive or over-bearing, or to infringe on the rights of other family members and peers, all in the name of exploring their creativity. In Chapter Six you will find tips on how to foster creativity in children by giving them the space they need, while at the same time enabling yourself to run a smooth, productive, and loving household.

All one needs to do is open a daily newspaper or listen to the nightly news on television to see how much the world is changing. Modifications in social values, expectations, occupations, political issues, environmental needs, medical advances, and even types of criminal behavior are evident. Your child will have to face a society filled with ever-changing challenges, and you will be doing your youngster a great service by providing the strategies to meet those challenges. Creative thinking and creative action are the most important tools your child can have in order to face the future in a competent and successful manner.

A Conversation About Creativity

Hap Palmer is an innovator in the use of music and movement to teach basic skills and encourage the use of imagination and creativity. Hap is a musician, singer, and educator whose goals are to write and record songs that reflect children's experiences and make learning enjoyable.

For more than twenty years, Hap's recordings have been widely used in schools and day care centers. His recordings and videos have received numerous honors, including the Parents' Choice Award, the American Library Association Notable Recording designation, and the American Video

Award. He also conducts workshops and presents concerts throughout the nation and has taught courses for various education extension programs. His educational background includes a master's in dance education from UCLA.

Q: *How and why did you start writing and performing music for children?*

A: As a classroom teacher, I wanted to create music that children could participate in actively—music they could sing and move with. I also found that active participation was an effective way to reinforce the school curriculum, so I wrote many songs which involve children in activities such as moving and naming body parts, identifying directions, as well as learning colors, numbers, and letters of the alphabet.

After twenty years of writing songs for use in classrooms and day care centers, I expanded into creating music for audio and video cassettes that children and parents could enjoy in the home setting.

Q: *Why is music important in children's lives?*

A: Music is an important part of the human experience and children should be exposed to music at a young age, along with other creative activities such as art and dance. We need to introduce children to a variety of artistic forms, then allow them to choose and pursue what catches their fancy.

The arts are not isolated subjects. They relate to other areas of a child's growth and development. Music can involve the whole child—mentally, physically, and emotionally. It can also aid in the development of motor skills, language, and creativity.

Q: *What does creativity mean to you?*

A: Flexibility, curiosity, open-mindedness. The ability to see different options and solutions to problems, and to see a variety of ways tasks can be accomplished. It's a way of thinking that includes not only the arts and literature but also science, mathematics, and everyday life situations.

Q: *Did you exhibit qualities of creativity as a child?*

A: I was fond of asking questions that began with "What if…?" Things like, "What if we attached wings to the car and drove real fast, would we fly?" or "What if I wrapped myself up in mattresses and jumped from the top of the house?" I would string these ideas together ad nauseam until one or both my parents would say, "What if you stopped talking and finished your dinner?"

I started lessons on the clarinet and saxophone when I was nine years old. By seventh and eighth grade I was playing in bands and small combos. I really enjoyed improvising, responding to chord progressions, and creating melodies. I was playing by ear and only later in college began to learn the theory of harmony. I realized there is a balance between knowledge and intuition; they are equally important in the creative act.

Q: *What did your parents do to encourage your creative abilities?*

A: I remember my parents encouraging creativity by not meddling or fussing over me much. I had great amounts of unstructured time and a garage full of things that I could fiddle with, things like tools, wood, wire, parts of old pinball machines, electrical gadgets (old motors, record players, amplifiers, speakers), and screws, bolts, and nails of every size. My father had all these things organized, sorted, and labeled in boxes. Much to his understandable annoyance, I never learned to put things away. We also had boxes of old clothes and a large collection of records—jazz, swing, classical, and musicals—I was free to play.

There were times when my parents would discourage creativity. I liked to invent and make my own gifts, things like a flower inside an empty toilet paper spool attached to a wood base. My mother finally told me one day that these were not real gifts. They were just junk.

Another time my sister and I were making up a play with some neighborhood friends. We were laughing and jabbering away, wearing old clothes we'd found in the garage, when my mother suddenly came in and got very upset. Her reason? We were ruining the things she'd saved to give away to Goodwill.

Looking back on these memories, the main thing I would tell parents is to relax. If a child has a drive to create, nothing you can do will stop it. So why not encourage creativity?

Q: *What did your teachers do?*

A: Creativity and imagination were not encouraged in my early school years. I struggled to focus my mind and learn basic skills, which I realize as an adult are also necessary for creative pursuits. My kindergarten teacher sent a note home to my parents saying that I was one of her problems. She wrote, "Hap is interested in everything, and can apply himself to nothing."

When I was in third or fourth grade, we had a

school talent show. I had nothing prepared, but I had a sudden spontaneous urge to get up onstage. Claiming I had a comedy act, I got up and started improvising. I ran over to a speaker and said, "This needs fixing." I got inside the enclosure and pantomimed wiggling wires. Then I pretended to get an electric shock. I leapt back and rolled all over the stage. As all the children laughed, the teacher came up and pulled me off the stage, saying something like, "You don't know what you're doing." This, of course, was true, but it could have been an opportunity to show how one moves from the brainstorming phase of creativity to act on an idea.

Q: *Was there anyone else who was a major influence on your creativity? How so?*

A: I met the people who had the biggest influence through books. In junior high school I enjoyed reading biographies, and many of them were about creative people. I was especially fascinated with Will Rogers and Thomas Edison. I took hope from the fact that Edison, like myself, was a poor student. Books gave me insight into how creative people worked.

Q: *Are there any special activities you would recommend to parents to foster creative thought and action in their children?*

A: Provide opportunities for exploring and experimenting. Have lots of materials available for children to choose from. Some examples:

Arts and crafts: paper, felt tip pens, clay

Drama: kitchen utensils, old pans, plastic dishes, old clothes in a costume box for playing make-believe

Music: rhythm sticks, tambourine, drum, woodblock, triangle, bells, cassette player with recordings of a variety of musical styles

Dance: provide young children with opportunities for movement exploration, rather than emphasizing competitive sports and formalized dance training

As children mature, let them choose the disciplines that catch their interest. Take children to classes and lessons when they are interested and when they ask for them.

Q: *Any other helpful hints for parents?*

A: Recognize that creativity often occurs in stages. First is preparation, when children become familiar with materials by exploring and discovering. This is followed by the generation of ideas, or brainstorming. For a free flow of ideas, don't pass judgments during these processes. Let evaluations come primarily from the child.

Creativity is a peculiar paradox of both freedom and discipline. There are techniques and principles inherent in any pursuit, which enhance and guide the creative impulse, and creative bursts often follow periods of patient, persistent effort.

Ideally, the discipline should come from within the child. As children mature, let them delve into what excites and interests them. Children are more likely to excel in those pursuits that are chosen by them rather than those imposed by adults.

Q: *Are there any particular resources you would suggest to parents?*

A: There are many excellent books on creativity that will help you evaluate programs and classes you are considering for your child. Three I particularly recommend are: *Creativity Is Forever* by Gary A. Davis (1983, Kendall/Hunt Publishing Co.); *Imagination* by Harold Rugg (1963, Harper & Row); and *Teaching; From Command to Discovery* by Muska Mosston (1972, Wadsworth Publishing Co.).

Where to Go for More Information on Creativity

* Amerikaner, S. Illustrated by T. Gleason (1989). *101 Things to Do to Develop Your Child's Gifts & Talents*. New York: Tom Doherty Associates (grades K–4). Fun activities that foster creative and critical thinking skills.
* *Communication Aids for Children and Adults* (1994). Catalog containing dozens of aids to enable children to develop communication skills, and physical challenges to expand their communication and creativity.
  > Crestwood Co.
  > 6625 N. Sidney Pl.
  > Milwaukee, WI 53209-3259
  > (414) 352-5678
* *Constructive Playthings*. Catalog has great selection of manipulatives, arts and crafts materials, multicultural books, pretend play materials, and much, much more.
  > Constructive Playthings
  > 1227 E. 119th St.
  > Grandview, MO 64030
  > (800) 448-4115
  > FAX: (816) 761-9295

• Gardner, H. (1983). *Frames of Mind: The Theory of Multiple Intelligences*. New York: Basic Books. Puts forth theory that there are multiple intelligences or areas of strength where individuals can excel.

• Guilford, J. P. (1967). *The Nature of Human Intelligence*. New York: McGraw-Hill. Describes the structure of the Intellect Model, a classification system that organizes 120 possible abilities according to the types of mental operations employed, the contents involved in the process, and the products that result from the act of thinking.

• Feldman, D. H., with L. T. Goldsmith (1990). *Nature's Gambit: Child Prodigies and the Development of Human Potential*. Scholarly analysis of the lives of six child prodigies.

> Teachers College Press
> P. O. Box 20
> Williston, VT 05495
> (800) 488-2665
> FAX: (802) 864-7626

• Hoot, J. L., & S. B. Silvern (1988). *Writing with Computers in the Early Grades*. National leaders in the field of computer applications in early childhood provide information on which software materials are most effective in helping children become better writers.

> Teachers College Press
> P. O. Box 20
> Williston, VT 05495
> (800) 488-2665
> FAX: (802) 864-7626

• National Research Center on the Gifted and Talented, The. *The National Research Center on the Gifted and Talented Newsletter*. Excellent articles dealing with all aspects of gifted and talented education, including the development and assessment of creativity.

> NRC/GT
> The University of Connecticut
> 362 Fairfield Rd., U-7
> Storrs, CT 06269-2007

- Roedell, W. C., N. E. Jackson & H. B. Robinson (1980). *Gifted Young Children*. Review of the literature on what is known about intellectual abilities and social development of gifted preschool and primary-grade children.

> Teachers College Press
> P. O. Box 20
> Williston, VT 05495
> (800) 488-2665
> FAX: (802) 864-7626

- Ward, W. (1952). *Stories to Dramatize*. Anchorage, KY: The Children's Theatre Press. A collection of poems and stories that are easy to dramatize. A classic in the field of creative drama.

Books to Help Foster Creativity

Barrett, S. L. (1992). *It's All in Your Head: A Guide to Understanding Your Brain and Boosting Your Brain Power*. Minneapolis: Free Spirit Publishing (grades 3–7). Includes ways to increase your creativity.

Coles, J. & R. Budwig (1990). *The Book of Beads*. New York: Simon & Schuster (grades 4 and up). A magnificent book that is sure to spark the imagination.

Edge, N. Illustrated by P. M. Leitz (1975). *Kids in the Kitchen*. Port Angeles, Wash.: Peninsula Publishing, Inc. (preschool–grade 4). Cookbook for children.

Epstein, D. & M. Safro (1991). *Buttons*. New York: Harry N. Abrams, Inc. (grades 4 and up). Beautiful reproductions tell the story of the history of buttons.

Jayne, C. F. (1962). *String Figures and How to Make Them*. (grades 4 and up). Thorough introduction to the study of string figures. New York: Dover Publication, Inc.

Kaplan, P., S. Crawford & S. Nelson (1987). *Creative Written Expression for Children*. Denver: Love Publishing Co. (grades 4–6). Creative writing activities.

Kramer, S. P. Illustrated by F. Bond (1987). *How to Think Like a Scientist: Answering Questions by the Scientific Method*. New York: Thomas Y. Crowell (grades 2–6). Fun way to teach your child about scientific thinking.

Lepscky, Ibi. *Pablo Picasso* (1984). New York: Barron's (grades 1–4).

McCoy, S. Illustrated by C. Olexiewicz (1994). *50 Nifty Friendship Bracelets, Rings & Other Things*. Los Angeles: Lowell House Juvenile (grades 4–6). Fun, unique gifts to make for friends.

Perl, T. (1993). *Women and Numbers: Lives of Women Mathematicians*. San Carlos, Calif.: Wide World Publ./Tetra (grades 5–9). Eleven profiles of female mathematicians and computer scientists. Geared for older children, but included here because there is a paucity of material in this area. May be easily adapted for younger children.

Pomaska, A. (1984). *Color Your Own Ready-to-Mail Postcards*. New York: Dover Publications, Inc. (grades K–3).

Santrey, L. Illustrated by S. Speidel (1986). *Louisa May Alcott*. Mahwah, N. J.: Troll Associates (grades 2–5). Young writer. Biography.

Supraner, R. & R. Barto (1981). *Great Masks to Make*. Mahwah, N. J.: Troll Associates (grades K–3).

Tison, C. & M. J. Woodside (1991). *Ultimate Collection of Computer Facts and Fun: A Kid's Guide to Computers*. Carmel, Ind.: Sams/Macmillan Computer Publishing (grades 3–6). Includes lots of goodies, from how a computer works to creating a spreadsheet.

Woodruff, E. *The Wing Shop* (1991). New York: Holiday House (grades 1–5). Story about a store filled with wings of all kinds. Great for fostering imagination.

Zakon, M. Illustrated by L. Feld & D. Liff (1991). *The Kids' Kosher Cookbook*. Southfield, Mich.: Targum/Feldheim (grades K–4).

Computer Software
That Encourages Creativity

Much of the computer software for children that fosters creativity comes out of the educational market. Listed below are some of the best of the most recent programs, most of which are award winners. All can be purchased from Edmark, P.O. Box 3218, Redmond, WA 98073-3218, (800) 362-2890, FAX: (206) 556-8430.

ColorMe: The Computer Coloring Kit (1987, 1985). Mindscape, Inc. (grades K–5). Flexible drawing and coloring program allows children to create and print their own pictures, coloring books, cards, stickers, and buttons.
Apple System Requirements: Apple II+, IIe, IIc, IIGS; 128K; 5¼" disk drive; mouse or joystick. Optional: TouchWindow, printer.
IBM/Compatible System Requirements: DOS 2.1 or higher; 256K; CGA or EGA. Optional: printer.

Cotton Tales Series (1993). Parent's Choice Golden Award. Mindplay (grades pre-K–2). (1) *Cotton Tales*, a desktop publishing and word processing program for children just learning to write; includes graphics, a dictionary, and a translator that converts pictures into words; (2) *Cotton Plus*, a library of colorful pictures to use with *Cotton Tales*; and (3) *Cotton Works*, a series of worksheets.

Macintosh System Requirements: MacPlus or better; 1 Mb for monochrome, 2 Mb for color; hard disk; digitized speech with System 6.0.7 or better. Optional: TouchWindow, printer (Mac version does not include Cotton Works).

Apple System Requirements: Apple II+, IIe, IIc, IIGS; 64K; 5¼" disk drive. Optional: printer.

IBM/Compatible System Requirements: 128K; color graphics card & color monitor; 5¼" or 3½" disk drive (both disks included). Optional: printer.

Easy Book (1993). Chickadee Software, Inc. (grades K–6). Allows children to write, illustrate, and publish their own books, complete with cover and title page. Exciting program.

Macintosh System Requirements: Macintosh Plus or higher; System 6.0 or higher; hard disk or two 800K disk drives; 1 Mb for monochrome, 2 Mb for color, 4 Mb for System 7.0 or later. Optional: TouchWindow.

Just Grandma & Me (1993, 1992, 1983). Broderbund (grades pre-K–2). Created by award-winning author & illustrator Mercer Mayer. An interactive reading trip to the beach. Multilingual (English, Spanish, and Japanese). Encourages thinking skills. Technology & Learning's 1992–1993 Award of Excellence.

Macintosh System Requirements: Macintosh LC or higher; System 6.0.7 or higher; 4 Mb; 256 color monitor; CD-ROM drive–4 MB–8 bit color card (256 colors). Optional: TouchWindow.

IBM/Compatible System Requirements: IBM or compatible 386SX or higher; Windows 3.1 and DOS 3.3 or higher; 4 Mb; Super VGA; mouse; Sound Blaster and compatible sound cards; CD-ROM drive (150KB per second or faster). Optional: TouchWindow.

Kid Pix (1991). Broderbund (grades K–6). A fun, free-form paint program that stimulates creativity. Includes recording capabilities, plus a talking dictionary in Spanish and English. High/Scope's Best Early Childhood Software Award and Educational Research Foundation Award for 1992; Technology and Learning's 1991–1992 Award of Excellence.

Macintosh System Requirements: Requires two–800K disk drives or a hard disk; MacRecorder optional; System 6.0; 1 Mb for monochrome, 2 Mb for color; System 7–2 Mb for monochrome, 4 Mb for color. Optional: TouchWindow, printer.

IBM/Compatible System Requirements: EGA, VGA, MCGA, Tandy 16-color compatible; 640K memory; Supports Sound Blaster, Tandy Sound, PS/1 and Disney Sound Source. Optional: TouchWindow, printer, sound card.

Treehouse (1991). Broderbund (grades K–4). Seven captivating games that encourage creativity, science skills, strategic thinking, and exploration, among other things. Amusing animation, sound effects, and activities. High/Scope's Best Early Childhood Software Award for 1992; Technology and Learning's 1992–1993 Award of Excellence.

Macintosh System Requirements: Macintosh Plus or higher; System 6.0.7 or higher; 2 Mb for monochrome, 4 Mb for color (for System 7.0, 4 Mb for monochrome and 5 Mb for color); hard disk. Optional: TouchWindow, printer.

IBM/Compatible System Requirements: IBM or compatible; 640K; EGA, VGA, or MCGA; 3½" disk drive; hard disk. Optional: TouchWindow, printer, sound card.

Apple System Requirements: Apple IIe, IIc, IIGS; 128K; 5¼" disk drive. Optional: printer.

·4·

The Gift of Social Consciousness

There is no higher religion
than human service. To work for
the common good is the
greatest creed. [30]

Albert Schweitzer,
French physician and humanitarian,
recipient of the Nobel Peace Prize

What do we mean by social consciousness?

One of the most treasured and welcomed gifts your child can possess is the ability to be interested in and compassionate about the larger world, as opposed to being concerned solely with her or his immediate surroundings and happenings. When this interest and concern is coupled with a willingness to become involved because of a desire to make the world a better place, then you have what is referred to as **social consciousness**.

Children are expected to begin to care about the outer world during the elementary school years. Although children of this age tend to be egocentric and generally feel the world revolves around them and their needs, this is also the age when young people tend to broaden their outlook. They begin to show interest in what is occurring in other places to other people, especially situations that have a direct or at least an indirect effect on them. Take a situation where a community is in an uproar over a proposed local development project, for example. This project is part of the outer world, yet children can relate to the probable increase of traffic in the neighborhood, which may lengthen their drive to school. The situation is one with which they can identify because the controversy has some type of direct effect on their lives.

During this period of development young people also gradually begin to show interest in the events of the outer world even if there is no link to their own lives. This is sometimes noticed by parents in a sporadic or piecemeal fashion. For instance, a news story seen on television about a political crisis in a faraway country, or the topic of gender discrimination in another culture brought up by a teacher, may suddenly spark the interest of a second or third grader.

Social consciousness becomes extraordinary when children of this age demonstrate a passion and commitment to get involved, make things better, and "heal the world." All children should be given an opportunity to develop their concern for the outer world. For those children who manifest a particular strength in this area, however, parents not only should put a great deal of effort into encouraging this area of growth, but they also should be shouting "Hallelujah!" from the rooftops. Social consciousness is a precious jewel, a highly valued gift to be celebrated with joy.

Did you know? Frederick Douglass (1817–1895) was America's most famous black abolitionist orator. He was editor of his own newspaper, the first black member of the electoral college, and the U.S. ambassador to Haiti.

This chapter will provide you with hints on how to identify and help develop social consciousness in your children. Furthermore, it will provide useful information for *all* parents on how to foster social concern in their children.

Is your child an especially socially conscious person?

One of the easiest ways to determine if your youngster is particularly strong in the area of social concern is to listen to the topics of conversation initiated by your child. Which topics pique her or his interest? It is extremely natural for children of elementary school age to spend much of their time talking about apparently silly topics. It is not uncommon for children to chatter endlessly about jokes they've heard from their friends, funny plots from their favorite television shows, goofy anecdotes about what happened at school, or just how "stupid" so-and-so is. These are necessary conversational topics for children. They are practicing their verbal skills, testing their powers of communication, and learning how they fit in to this crazy thing called life. By listening carefully to what children have to say, you can discover whether social issues are particularly important to them.

Observe how your child behaves in certain situations. Do you notice a general *caring* attitude? Take note of those activities that motivate or interest your youngster (remember your role as anthropologist from Chapter One).

How do others perceive your child? As discussed in Chapter Two, you can gain great insight by carefully watching how other people act toward your daughter or son. A particular characteristic or trait may be more apparent to peers or to other adults than to you as a parent.

Let's say you are trying to assess how socially concerned your daughter Kim is. Here are some questions you may want to ask yourself:

- Does Kim seem to have a heightened sense of "fairness"?
- Does she voluntarily watch the news on television or read parts of the newspaper?
- Does she ask questions about current political or social situations? If you bring up this type of topic, does she seem interested?
- Is she concerned about those who are less fortunate than she is?
- Does she ask how she can help others? Does she come up with ideas on her own?
- Do adults describe Kim as a kind, generous, or compassionate person?

- When she is writing a story or a poem for school, does she choose topics that contain elements of social concern, such as poverty or discrimination?
- Does she demonstrate empathy? In other words, is she moved by the suffering or plight of others?
- Does she include the poor, the homeless, or unwanted pets in her evening prayers?
- Does she want to give money when the two of you are confronted by a homeless person on the street asking for change?
- When she's playing a board game with friends, is she especially generous to the person who is clearly losing? ("Here, you can have one of my chips.")
- Does she seem to get as much, or more, pleasure from giving gifts as she does from receiving them?
- Is she thoughtful?
- Does she try to rescue stray animals?

No child, of course, is expected to demonstrate all the above characteristics. What you want to look for is a pattern or cluster of such behaviors.

How can you help your child develop social consciousness?

Modeling, or observational learning, has long been recognized as playing a major role in what children learn and how they develop.[31] The most effective way to develop social consciousness in your child is to model such behavior. Children need to see social concern in action. When they witness people whom they admire, such as parents, older siblings, or teachers, behaving in ways that manifest a concern for others, they are seeing behavior that they are likely to emulate.

There are many ways for you, as a parent, to model socially conscious behavior. Some may be clearly indicative of social concern. You may choose to volunteer as a listener for a local crisis hotline, donate food and clothing, visit a nursing home during the holidays, become involved in local community politics, discuss socially relevant topics as a family, or faithfully recycle. However, there are many other ways, perhaps more subtle, that also demonstrate a concern for others. For example, you may refuse to use pesticides in the garden or to repeat

Generally, if you are kind, your child will be kind.

jokes that ridicule people with disabilities or people from other cultures and races. You may pick up trash along the roadside, adopt a pet from a local shelter, or be a courteous driver. Realizing that children are incredibly observant, and utilizing this characteristic, is the most important thing you can do to foster socially conscious behavior in your child. You are your child's ultimate teacher.

Get actively involved in what is happening at your child's school. Many middle and secondary schools and a few elementary schools are including community service projects as part of their curriculum. If your child's school does not offer this component, why not speak to the faculty and other parents about starting one? Community projects are organized activities where young people are involved in being of service to others. Although some projects may be done on campus, students often leave the school grounds and work out in the community. Such activities include helping teachers at childcare centers; giving to those in need; entertaining at local special education centers, nursing homes, and hospitals; offering assistance to animal rescue organizations; or planting trees for a neighborhood environmental group. Why not offer your time to help with the organization of the activities? If you are a working parent without much free time, you might consider offering to make phone calls, address envelopes, or copy fliers as your contribution. You may even get your child to help you. If your job involves some aspect of social concern, you might consider speaking to your child's class about how your company helps others, or inviting the class to your place of work as a field trip.

Utilizing children's literature that contains caring themes has long been encouraged by educators in the classroom.[32] Emphasizing this type of literature in the home is another way for parents to encourage social consciousness. At the end of this chapter you will find a listing of books (plus movies on video) currently on the market that contain socially responsible messages. The important thing is to help your child discover the themes inherent in the books. For example, if you are reading a story with your son about a little boy who does a good deed, you can ask, "How would you feel if you were that little boy?" or "What do you think would happen if he hadn't done what he did?" These types of open-ended questions will allow you to have a creative dialogue with your youngster. They will foster empathy and help your child explore the area of kindness and its consequences.

Another way to encourage social consciousness is to value diversity in your home. Diversity here refers to people from other cultures; people with differences, such as disabilities and those who speak other languages; and people of all ages, religions, sexual orientations, and occupations.

Let's look at the area of disabilities as an example. According to the 15th Annual Report to Congress, approximately five million students, or 10 percent of the student population ages 6–17, received special education services during the 1991–1992 school year.[33] Of these students, 94.4 percent were educated at a regular school campus, and 69.3

percent were educated in a regular classroom more than 40 percent of their instructional time. This is great news. It means that in all likelihood your child, who may or may not be disabled, will at some time have peers in her or his classroom who have disabilities. What a marvelous opportunity for your youngster to be exposed to differences! Show your enthusiasm for having children with visual or hearing problems, learning or behavioral difficulties, or complex health needs as classmates of your child. You will be demonstrating how much you value diversity. The classroom will be a richer place because of its diversity and will contribute to your child's development as a caring and socially conscious individual. Suggest that children with special needs be included in playtime activities. Reach out and talk to these children's parents, and encourage open discussion in your own family about differences.

There are many children's books currently on the market that deal directly with young people who have disabilities. An increasing number of portrayals of these children depict them mainstreamed into regular education classrooms, meaning that they spend at least part of the school day with nondisabled peers. When they spend an entire school day in such classrooms, the arrangement is called "full inclusion." Please note that it helps to peruse such books before or while your youngster is reading them. Even some well-meaning books may provide inaccurate information or put forth an attitude with which you disagree. They may even confuse your child, or the graphics may perpetuate undesirable stereotypes and generalizations. A cute storyline and interesting characters do not preclude the possibility that an inappropriate portrayal of children with disabilities may hurt rather than enhance your child's understanding of differences.[34]

If you find that the book in question is faulty in some of

The Me Puzzle

When speaking to your child about disabilities, it is wise to emphasize the similarities among people, and to point out that even children with severe impairments possess strengths and talents. Do you need a fun, wonderful activity for a rainy day or a long car ride? Here's one that reinforces the idea that we are all complex individuals with many different components to our lives. Most areas of our lives run fairly smoothly, but we all have an area or two where things may not be going as well as we would like.

Encourage your child to draw an empty jigsaw puzzle on a piece of paper, initially leaving all the pieces blank. Ask your youngster to write something good about her or his life on each piece except one. In other words, one piece is left blank. When she or he gets to that point, ask the child to fill in the last piece with one thing in her or his life that isn't perfect, is not going well, or needs help. You might want to do the activity with your child, make your own Me Puzzle, and compare them. Then, using a familiar person or character from a book, movie, or television show, explain that even a person with a disability has many things that are good in her or his life. A disability, no matter how severe, is still just one small part of who a person is.

This activity can be used with groups of children, so if your child has friends over to play, why not give it a try? You'll be amazed at the types of topics that children bring up. "Good things" can include getting 100 percent on a math test, having Joey as a best friend, or getting the highest score on a computer game. The things that are "not so good" could be anything from having a fight with a friend or wearing a hearing aid to having to go to the hospital for an operation. Children love talking about themselves, and the topic of differences can be discussed in a playful and interesting way. (We all know how young people dislike preaching!)

the above-mentioned areas, it can still be used as a spring-board to a healthy discussion concerning what *is* wrong with the portrayal. For example, is the person with a disability shown in only passive, rather than active, roles? Would a reader of the book who was disabled find the portrayal unrealistic or insulting? The same principles hold true for videos, movies, and television shows. At the end of this chapter you will find a compilation of books and films currently available that deal with disabilities and are appropriate for elementary-age children.

Another way to show that you, as a parent, value diversity is to speak with respect about others. As mentioned earlier, the language that people use has an uncanny knack of reflecting and shaping how they think and feel. It is a cyclical relationship. One way to use respectful language is to speak of people as individuals first, as opposed to always being referred to as members of a particular group. This way of describing people emphasizes the notion that individuals are not the sum of their group membership. Rather, they are full, interesting individuals who happen to also belong to a particular group or groups of like persons.

Social consciousness can be further fostered by helping your child discover the myriad choices available for involvement, and then helping her or him learn how to get involved. If your youngest daughter, Michelle, feels passionate about helping animals, you might want to help her discover which local organizations would welcome a child visitor or volunteer. Perhaps she might prefer to raise money to buy a book or two about endangered species to donate to her school library. She may decide to raise the necessary money by organizing a neighborhood bake sale, or getting friends together for a used-toy drive. Instead, your daughter may love to draw and may decide to ask the principal of her school to allow her to put up animal rights posters around the school campus. Whatever the activity, it is most important that the area of involvement and the specific way that Michelle gets involved are chosen by her, not Mom or Dad. Parents are best at gently facilitating or helping the process.

There are several suggestions to keep in mind. One is to encourage Michelle to do as much of the work herself as possible. Give only minimal assistance. After all, it may be *her* cause and not necessarily yours. Another is to guide Michelle into activities that can realistically be done by a child. Sometimes children take on more than they can handle. If they try to tackle a huge job and fail, they can easily become discouraged and frustrated. It is much better if they take on a project that has a realistic chance of being completed successfully. It is wise to keep an eye on the situation, periodically assessing how the project is going. Of course, you will want to help, but again, only when needed.

Not only does involvement in such activities encourage social consciousness, but many skills that are necessary for success inside and outside of school can also be developed. A few such skills are

- how to write a letter
- how to organize materials
- how to manage time
- how to verbally communicate ideas clearly
- how to research an idea
- where to go for information
- how to recruit others to join a project
- how to plan an activity from start to finish
- what to do when things go wrong.

Do some of these skills sound familiar? Many of the skills used in manifesting social consciousness are also needed for leadership and creativity. This demonstrates one of the marvelous benefits of developing gifts and talents. When strengths are nurtured in one area, the positive effects flow over and influence other areas of functioning. For example, an added bonus to Michelle's involvement with animals could be that her self-concept is given a healthy boost because she is successfully accomplishing something positive to make the world a better place. What could be more wonderful?

Respect for the environment is another aspect of social consciousness that deserves to be explored. Theoretically, one can have a strong concern about the affairs of the people of the world without being particularly interested in the actual state of the physical earth on which those people live. Likewise, one can feel passionate about protecting the environment while being generally uninterested in, or even disdainful of, its inhabitants. Most parents, however, hope to encourage an understanding of and love for all people, as well as a respect and sense of responsibility for the environment. Ideally, the two should go hand in hand.

By the time they reach the elementary school years, many children have already had several years of exposure to environmental problems and ecological issues, and they are bursting with enthusiasm to do something to help. Their idealism has not been dampened by the realities of life, as so

> To create and encourage an awareness among the people of the world of the need for wise use and proper management of those resources of the Earth upon which our lives and welfare depend: the soil, the air, the water, the forests, the minerals, the plant life, and the wildlife. [35] (Editorial Creed)
>
> Jay D. Hair, chairman, National Wildlife Federation

Suggested Activities That Foster Respect for the Environment

♦ George Bernard Shaw knew what he was talking about when he wrote that the best place to seek God is in a garden.[36] **Designate a portion of your backyard, a few pots on the patio, or a window box as your child's own private garden.** Show your child how to use gardening books to find out the necessary information, such as which plants are appropriate during certain times of the year, and which plants grow best in sun or shade. Success is more likely if children start with seedlings as opposed to seeds. However, there's nothing like the satisfaction that your child will feel when she or he has grown a lovely plant from a single seed. You might want to compromise and suggest that your youngster plant both seedlings and seeds. Having both edibles and nonedibles, along with fast-growing and slow-growing plants, is also a wise idea. Children absolutely love owning their own things. How about buying a set of gardening tools for your child's next birthday? You'll be giving a present that is durable, appreciated, and sure to get much use.

♦ Why fight television? It's here to stay. The trick is to make television work *for* you, not *against* you. **Utilize commercials.** Have your child pick out a commercial for a particular product. Suggest that your daughter or son make a list of all the ways that the manufacturing and use of the product helps the environment and hurts the environment.

- Ask your youngster to think up a new product that would be good for the environment. **Suggest creating a commercial or jingle** to market the product. If you have a video recorder, you can tape the exercise for your child. Better yet, suggest this activity when friends are over. Let your child do the taping. (Supervision may be necessary!)

- Present your child with a fact, such as:

  Every year approximately one billion pounds of pesticides are applied to crops in the United States at the cost of more than $4 billion.[37]

  Suggest your child write and design a comic strip or draw a poster about this fact. The finished product can be displayed at home or shared at school.

- **Help your child locate photographs of your neighborhood or community taken many years ago** (neighbors, your local library, and your city's historical society are good resources). Discuss the changes that have taken place. It will become clearer just how mankind affects the world when your child sees the present-day gas station where oak trees once grew, or the paved street where a rolling hillside used to be. You can also have your child locate and interview a senior citizen who has lived in the neighborhood for a long time. This is another way to understand the changes that have taken place in a specific environment.

- If there is an environmental issue in which your child shows interest, **encourage and help her or him to write a letter of concern** to the appropriate company, politician, or local newspaper. Suggest that some personal information (such as school or extra-curricular activities) be included in the letter along with the environmental subject matter. Recipients of such letters tend to pay more attention to corres-pondence that has a warm, personal touch than to a cold form letter. Also, your child will more likely get a response if bits of personal information are included.

- **Encourage respect for food.** Leftovers on the plate can be minimized by suggesting that family members take smaller portions at a time. Leftovers can also be recycled as compost for the garden. (You might even want to order special worms to help you with this one![38] Worms can be purchased from bait dealers, usually listed in phone books under the heading *Fishing Bait*, or ordered directly from commercial growers who advertise in gardening and fishing magazines.) Encourage your child not to use food products for art projects (use beads instead of macaroni, for example). When food shopping together, show your concern for what you eat by checking the ingredients of products. Better yet, why not let your youngster be in charge and be the one to read the labels?

- **Live a life in which bigger doesn't always mean better, and more isn't always preferred.** It is healthy for children to grow up in families where unchecked consumerism and the never-ending quest for material possessions are not the ultimate goals. Why not recycle old books and toys by having your child organize an exchange with classmates or neighborhood buddies?

- **Help your child start a neighborhood beautification project.** Picking up trash, planting appropriate plants and trees, and making small repairs will prove extremely satisfying to your daughter or son. It can also be a great way to get to know your neighbors and have fun at the same time.

- In *Education Goes Outdoors*, the authors suggest you **take your child on a sidewalk expedition.**[39] Examine how the concrete affects the nearby natural environment. Are there places where plants are growing up through the cracks? Are the roots of a nearby tree pushing up the concrete? Is an anthill visible alongside the sidewalk? Does it appear that the paving of the sidewalk modified the natural shape of the land? This activity will help your child see the relationship between mankind and nature.

often happens with adults. A logical consequence of this desire is an active involvement in working toward protecting our natural resources. This is usually referred to as **environmental activism**. Such activism needs to be based on an understanding of one's interactions with one's surrounding environment. In other words, children must interact with their immediate environment and understand those interactions before they can develop the desire to protect the environment on a grander scale.

Children enjoy being involved. They are doers. Youngsters also love the act of discovery. They are explorers, learners, and detectives. Environmental activism is a perfect match between these natural instincts and the developmental level of young people in the elementary years.

One final way to encourage social consciousness is to let your child know that her or his efforts can make a difference. One of the best resources available in this area is Barbara Lewis's *The Kid's Guide to Social Action*.[40] This book is chock-full of ways to turn ideas of social concern into successful plans of action. The author covers everything from initiating and changing laws and effectively using the media to meet objectives, to writing newspaper editorials and grant proposals. Her advice to children is a good reminder to parents, as well:

> *You have the right to shape your future.*
> *Don't wait for someone else to do it for you.*
> *Speak up. Speak out.*
> *Design a world you want to live in.*
> *Don't wait for luck to create it.*
> *Luck is just another word for work.*
> *The world needs to see your works and to*
> *hear your voices.*

This chapter has given you hints on how to identify and

help develop social consciousness in your child. If your child has not shown an interest in social concern, you can help cultivate this quality in your youngster. Social consciousness is a gift that will benefit your child and will affect her or his relationship with your family, the country, and the world.

Conversations About Social Consciousness

To understand better how social consciousness affects people's lives, read the following conversation with **Carol Halperin,** a woman who has devoted her life to social service. She is Director of Community Service and One Voice Coordinator at Crossroads School for the Arts & Sciences, as well as a member of the St. Joseph Community Advisory Board. (For a description of the One Voice program, see page 94.)

Q: *How would you define social consciousness?*

A: I would describe it as the awareness of people and their environment.

Q: *Did you exhibit qualities of social consciousness as a child?*

A: Yes, I cared about other people. My mother was philanthropic, so I was raised wanting to do something for others. It was built into the way I live. It became part of me.

Q: *What did your parents do to encourage social consciousness when you were a child?*

A: They taught me by being involved themselves. They set a good example and encouraged me to join them in what they were doing, as well as to develop my own interests.

Q: *What did your teachers do to encourage social consciousness?*

A: I got nothing from school in this area that I can remember.

Q: *Are there any activities that you would recommend to parents to encourage social consciousness in their children?*

A: Family activities, community work, and simple things like recycling...also, reading the paper and discussing issues of concern and talking about solutions.

Q: *Do you have any other tips for parents?*

A: Yes. Encourage your children, set examples, provide opportunities, and discuss social problems as a family.

Q: *Why do you think social consciousness is important?*

A: So people can relate, get along, understand, be sensitive to each other, and not be isolated from each other. It's important to realize that you can make a difference and influence other people to do the same.

Q: *What makes social consciousness special to you?*

A: Well, I have a sense of involvement and empowerment that I'm doing something about what needs to be done.

Q: *How has being socially conscious helped you and enhanced your life?*

A: It's brought me in contact with wonderful people, both those I've helped and those I've worked with in helping. It's given me direction and purpose.

The following is a conversation with another person who has dedicated her life to social service. **Susan Silbert** is founder and director of One Voice and also teaches sociology at California State University, Northridge.

Q: *Tell me about your organization, One Voice.*

A: One Voice is a community-oriented, grassroots organization that tries to provide avenues of involvement to help people in need in our community. There are many programs to allow low-income families to have the same opportunities as others. We try to establish a human family, care for each other, help one another, learn about one another, and live well together.

Q: *What does social consciousness mean to you?*

A: It means caring for other people and basically having a true sense of morality. I define morality as how you interact with other people and the environment: decency, compassion, and caring.

Q: *What first got you interested in community service?*

A: I have always been involved. I really can't remember when I wasn't involved in some way. Things always seemed unfair to me. We should all be a family.

Q: *Were you interested in helping others even as a child?*

A: Yes. There was one specific example I remember. I remember driving by the bus stop and seeing older women of color who were maids. They looked old and tired, and I felt strongly that they shouldn't have to work. I clearly remember wanting to help people close to home, as well as strangers.

Q: *Do you remember any specific ways that your parents encouraged you in the area of social consciousness?*

A: My father was a lawyer. He had a strong sense of justice, fairness, and ethics. My mother was a sensitive woman. They didn't directly help others like I do, but they presented a wonderful socially conscious atmosphere, a platform of values.

Q: *How about your teachers?*

A: I can't remember any way they encouraged me in this area.

Q: *Do you think things are changing with teachers?*

A: They certainly are. They're becoming more aware.

Q: *Do you have any suggestions for parents on how to foster social consciousness in their children?*

A: Basically, set an example. Don't be hypocrites; children can see right through that. Be honest in what you believe. Don't ask your children to be involved in something if you're not willing to be involved.

Q: *How has social consciousness helped you in your life?*

A: I was going to say it is my life, but it's really a large part of my life. It's always there in my relationships with others.

Q: *Is there anything else you'd like to share?*

A: Yes. We all need to assume responsibility. Get involved in something that has meaning to you. We can all do something.

Q: *Can you recommend any particular resources for parents?*

A: Resources are readily available if you want them. You can find them all around. If there is not an organization that fits what you're looking for, do something on your own. If you see homeless people, collect food in your neighborhood and donate it to an organization to help them. Resources and opportunities are everywhere.

Where to Go for More Information on Socially Relevant Issues

Animal Rights

American Society for the Prevention of Cruelty to Animals (ASPCA)
(national animal rights organization)

441 E. 92nd St.
New York, NY 10128
(800) 395-ASPCA
(212) 876-7700

Fox Cubs

(children's branch of British Hunt Saboteurs Association; provides information on vegetarianism and hunted animals; publishes Fox Cubs *newsletter [will send info pack with four newsletters for $5])*

> P.O. Box 1
> Carlton, Nottingham
> NG4 25Y
> England, U.K.

National Humane Education Society

(animal rights organization focusing on humane education and care of animals; publishes quarterly journal; offers free reprints of articles on a variety of animal welfare topics, such as a collection of Noah's News, *geared toward elementary school students)*

> 15-B Catoctin Circle SE, Suite 207
> Leesburg, VA 22075
> (703) 777-8319

People for the Ethical Treatment of Animals (PETA)

(national animal rights organization; offers children's newsletter [$3/year], PETA Kids*)*

> P.O. Box 42516
> Washington, DC 20015-0516
> Peta Merchandise:
> P.O. Box 42400
> Washington, DC 20015-0516

Student Action Corps for Animals (SACA)

(offers information on alternatives to dissection and how to organize a student group; publishes SACA News *newsletter)*

> P.O. Box 15588
> Washington, DC 20003-0588
> (202) 543-8983

Diversity—Disabilities

Advocates ◆ Resources ◆ Counseling

(coordinates a parent-to-parent support program; publishes a newsletter for parents and grandparents of children with special needs)

ARC of King County
2230 Eighth Ave.
Seattle, WA 98121
(206) 622-9324

Clearinghouse on the Handicapped

(many free services available to parents concerning information, referrals, and advocacy programs for individuals with disabilities)

Office of Special Education &
Rehabilitative Services
U.S. Department of Education
Switzer Bldg., Room 3132
Washington, DC 20202-2319
(202) 732-1214

Council for Exceptional Children

(major educational and advocacy group with specific divisions on all areas of exceptionality; excellent journals and conferences)

1920 Association Dr.
Reston, VA 22091
(703) 620-3660

National Handicapped Sports

(sponsors a variety of sports, recreation, and fitness programs for persons with disabilities)

451 Hungerford Dr., Suite 100
Rockville, MD 20850
(301) 217-0960
TDD: (301) 217-0963
FAX: (301) 217-0968

Sibling Info. Network

(national and international group for siblings, parents, and teachers interested in the special needs of families of persons with disabilities)

The A. J. Pappanikou Center
1776 Ellington Rd. S.
Windsor, CT 06074

Diversity—Other Cultures

Afro-Am Distributing Company

(great selection of books, games, and posters for children and adults on African-Americans and Africa)

819 South Wabash Ave.
Chicago, IL 60605

Anti-Defamation League of B'Nai B'rith

(resources and materials pertaining to multicultural issues, prejudice, discrimination, and the Holocaust)

Dept. JW
823 United Nations Plaza
New York, NY 11117
(212) 490-2525

Constructive Playthings

(special catalog: Culturally Diverse Materials for Anti-Bias Curriculums; great selection, everything from international toy food sets to culturally diverse musical instruments and books)

1227 E. 119th St.
Grandview, MO 64030
(800) 448-4115
FAX: (816) 761-9295

Migrant Education Resource List Information Network (MERLIN)

(disseminates information on the educational needs of migrant children)

MERLIN
Pennsylvania Department of Education
8th Floor, 333 Market St.
Harrisburg, PA 17018
(800) 233-0306
(717) 783-7121

National Association for Bilingual Education

(clearinghouse for information concerning bilingual education; publications provided)

Room 407, 1201 16th St., NW
Washington, DC 20036
(202) 822-7870

Environmental

Audubon Society

(provides information on organizing youth groups in environmental education)

950 Third Ave.
New York, NY 10022
(212) 832-3200

Environmental Defense Fund

(national advocacy group with goal of environmental protection)

257 Park Ave. South
New York, NY 10010
(212) 505-2100

Farm Animal Rangers (FAR)

(children's branch of Compassion in World Farming; publishes OUT magazine for youth)

> 20 Lavant Street
> Petersfield, Hampshire
> GU32 3EW
> England, U.K.

The Wilderness Society

(defends America's national forests, national parks, and other wild lands)

> 900 17th St., NW
> Washington, DC 20006-2596
> (202) 833-2300

Youth for Environmental Sanity (YES)

(environmental activism for children and adolescents)

> 706 Frederick St.
> Santa Cruz, CA 95062

Helping Others

Catholic Charities, USA

(official service center of the Catholic Church)

> 1319 F St., NW
> Washington, DC 20004
> (202) 639-8400

Church World Service

(mandated to inform and sensitize the U.S. public about the causes of hunger, the limitations of global resources, and the interdependence of all people)

> Office of Global Education
> 2115 N. Charles St.
> Baltimore, MD 21218
> (301) 727-6106

The Children's Defense Fund

(advocacy group for poor children, those from minority groups, and those with disabilities)

> 122 C St., NW, Suite 400
> Washington, DC 20001
> (202) 628-8787

Council of Jewish Federations

(represents Jewish social service organizations across the country)

> 227 Massachusetts Ave., NW
> Washington, DC 20002
> (202) 547-0020

HandsNet, Inc.

(national network for gathering information and resources dealing with fighting hunger, homelessness, and poverty)

> 303 Potrero St., Suite 54
> Santa Cruz, CA 95060
> (408) 427-0527

InterAction

(collects and disseminates information about volunteer organizations working on the problem of world hunger and the rights of children)

> 200 Park Ave. South
> New York, NY 10003
> (212) 777-8210

Literacy Volunteers of America

(national literacy group; trains volunteers)

> 5795 Widewaters Pkwy.
> Syracuse, NY 13214
> (315) 445-8000

National Alliance to End Homelessness

(largest organization dedicated to fighting homelessness; leading clearinghouse on information dealing with homelessness in America)

> 1518 K St., NW, Suite 206
> Washington, DC 20005
> (202) 638-1526

World Share

(community-based organization specializing in empowering individuals to help end hunger in America)

> 5255 Lovelock St.
> San Diego, CA 92110
> (619) 294-2981

Books With Themes of Social Concern

A plethora of books has been published dealing with how to help make the world a better place. These materials cover a wide range of topics, and many contain helpful hints that parents can use to learn more about how to develop social consciousness in their children. Others are aimed at children directly, including storybooks that contain themes of social consciousness.

Animal Rights

Adams, R. (1977). *The Plague Dogs.* New York: Fawcett Crest. Warm story about two dogs who are fugitives from an animal research laboratory.

Koebner, L. (1991). Illustrated by T. C. Whittemore. *For Kids Who Love Animals: A Guide to Sharing the Planet.* New York: Berkley Books.

Living Planet Press (1990). *The Animal Rights Handbook: Everyday Ways to Save Animal Lives.* Los Angeles: Author.

People for the Ethical Treatment of Animals (1994). *Shopping Guide for Caring Consumers.* Summertown, Tenn.: Author. A guide to products that are not tested on animals.

Diversity—Disabilities

Berkus, C. W. (1992). Photographed by M. Dodd. *Charlsie's Chuckle.* Rockville, Md.: Woodbine House, (800) 843-7323; FAX: (301) 468-5784. (grades K–6). Delightful story about a boy with Down's Syndrome.

Galvin, M. R. (1988). *Otto Learns About His Medicine: A Story About Medication for Hyperactive Children.* New York: Magination Press/Brunner/Mazel (ages K–3).

Moore, C. (1990). *A Reader's Guide: For Parents of Children with Mental, Physical, or Emotional Disabilities,* 3rd ed. Rockville, Md.: Woodbine House, (800) 843-7323; FAX: (301) 468-5784. Annotated bibliography of more than 1,000 books and other resources for parents.

Moss, D. (1989). Illustrated by C. Schwartz. *Lee, the Rabbit with Epilepsy.* Rockville, Md.: Woodbine House, (800) 843-7323; FAX: (301) 468-5784 (grades K–3). Beautiful tale of a rabbit with a seizure disorder.

Quinn, P. O. & J. Stern (1991). *Putting On the Brakes: Young People's Guide to Understanding Attention Deficit Hyperactivity Disorder (ADHD).* New York: Magination Press (grades 2–7).

Sanford, D. (1986). *Don't Look at Me.* Hong Kong: Multnomah Press (grades K–4). A child's viewpoint of being different (mental retardation).

Stern, J. M. & P. Quinn (1994). *Brakes. The Interactive Newsletter for Kids with ADHD*. New York: Brunner/Mazel (grades 1–8). Publication for children with attention deficit hyperactivity disorder, including suggested strategies, resources, and activities.

Thompson, M. (1992). *My Brother, Matthew*. Rockville, Md.: Woodbine House, (800) 843-7323; FAX: (301) 468-5784 (grades K–5). Realistic, loving story about family life centering around the needs of a child with a disability. Great for siblings.

Diversity—Other Cultures

Cameron, P. (1993). *Bridge Across Asia: Favorite Asian Stories*. San Diego: Dominie Press (grades 4–6).

Coerr, E. Illustrated by R. Himler (1977). *Sadako and the Thousand Paper Cranes*. New York: Bantam Doubleday Dell Publishing Group (grades 3–5). True story about a little girl who lived in Japan from 1943 to 1955 and was in Hiroshima when the U.S. dropped the atomic bomb.

Drucker, M. (1991). *Frida Kahlo*. New York: Bantam Books (grades 3–7). Includes several photographs of the painter and her work.

Feelings, T. (1993). *Soul Looks Back in Wonder*. New York: Dial Books. Contributions of African-American poetry from thirteen major poets, including Maya Angelou.

Filipovic, Zlata (1994). *Zlata's Diary: A Child's Life in Sarajevo*. New York: Viking Penguin. A thirteen-year-old's experiences of the war in Bosnia.

Ford, C. W. (1994). *We Can All Get Along: 50 Steps You Can Take to Help End Racism at Home, at Work, in Your Community*. New York: Dell Publishing.

Haskins, J. (1989). *Count Your Way Through Japan*. Minneapolis: Carolrhoda Books, Inc. Shows how to count in Japanese and other aspects of Japanese life. Series includes Korea, Mexico, China, Canada, and the Arab world.

Morris, A. Photographs by K. Heyman. *Bread, Bread, Bread* (1989), *Hats, Hats, Hats* (1992), *Houses and Homes* (1992), *Tools* (1992). New York: Lothrop, Lee & Shepard Books (grades K–3). Simple text and beautiful photographs depict everyday life in a variety of cultures.

Musgrove, M. Illustrated by L. & D. Dillon (1993). *Ashanti to Zulu: African Traditions*. New York: Dial (grades 2–5). Beautiful descriptions of twenty-six African tribes. Caldecott Medal winner.

Ryoff, A.L.B. (1991). *Literatures of the American Indian*. New York: Chelsea House (grades 3–7). Includes oratory, autobiographies, stories, and songs throughout history.

Thomson, B. J. (1993). *Words Can Hurt You: Beginning a Program of Anti-Bias Education*. Menlo Park, Calif.: Addison-Wesley. Excellent collection of activities for teachers to encourage cultural awareness and sensitivity to disabilities; also includes ways to examine prejudice and discrimination. Helpful for parents as well.

Yep, L. (1993). *Dragon's Gate*. New York: HarperCollins (grades 5–7; because there is a paucity of material in this area, recommended for even younger children if adapted). Story of a Chinese immigrant boy's struggles during the time of the American Civil War. Newbery Honor Book.

Environmental

Carter, F. (1976). *The Education of Little Tree*. New York: Delacorte. Boyhood of a Cherokee youth with emphasis on living a life close to nature.

Children of the World in Association with the United Nations (1994). *Rescue Mission: Planet Earth, A Children's Edition of Agenda 1*. New York: Kingfisher Books/Grisewood & Dempsey (grades 2–6). Colorful compilation of information on the "natural world" and the "human world."

Crowder, Jack (1986). *Tonibah and the Rainbow*. Bernalillo, N.M.: Upper Strata Ink, Inc. (grades 1–4). Story of a modern-day Navajo family. Written in both Navajo and English.

Javna, J. Illustrated by M. Montez (1994). *Fifty Simple Things Kids Can Do to Recycle*. The Earthworks Group. Berkeley: Earthworks Press (grades 2 and up).

MacGill-Calihan. Illustrated by B. Moser. (1991). *And Still the Turtle Watched*. New York: Dial (grades 1–4). Sweet story of ecological pollution and how it improved, centering around the experiences of a turtle.

Miles, B. (1991). *Save the Earth: An Action Handbook for Kids*. New York: Knopf (grades 4–12). Shows children how to transform thought to constructive action.

Rifkin, J. (1990). *The Green Lifestyle Handbook: 1001 Ways You Can Heal the Earth*. New York: Holt & Co.

Wilkes, A. (1991). Photographs by D. King & M. Dunning. *My First Green Book*. New York: Knopf (grades 2–5). A "how-to" book for children describing environmental problems and how to solve them.

Helping Others

Delisle, J. (1991). *Kid Stories: Biographies of 20 Young People You'd Like to Know*. Minneapolis: Free Spirit (grades 3–7). Inspiring accounts of young people who have done something to improve the world.

Home. *A Collaboration of 30 Distinguished Authors and Illustrators of Children's Books to Aid the Homeless*. (1992). New York: A Charlotte Zolotow Book/HarperCollins (grades 3 and up). Special project with proceeds going to Share Our Strength (SOS).

EarthWorks Group (1993). *You Can Change America*. Berkeley: Earthworks Press.

Eyre, L. & R. Eyre (1993). *Teaching Your Children Values*. New York: Simon & Schuster.

Haatkoff, A. & K. K. Klopp (1992). *How to Save the Children*. New York: Simon & Schuster. An innovative resource guide filled with practical ideas to counter the effects of poverty and neglect on America's children.

Kenyon, T. L., with J. Blau (1991). *What You Can Do to Help the Homeless*. New York: Simon & Schuster/Fireside.

Lewis, B. A. (1991). *The Kid's Guide to Social Action*. Minneapolis: Free Spirit (grades 4–12). Teaches children the necessary "power tools" to make a positive difference.

Films With Themes of Social Concern

Benny & Joon (1993). Uplifting story about people with mental illness. MGM. 98 min.

Ferngully: The Last Rainforest (1992). Powerful ecological message in a "politically correct" animated adventure. FAI. 76 min.

Flipper (1963). Boy saves injured dolphin. MGM. 87 min.

Free Willy (1993). Boy frees captured whale. Le Studio Canal Plus/Regency/Alcor. 111 min.

Into the West (1992). Children save horse. Beautifully photographed. Majestic/FFI/Miramax/Newcom/Little Bird. 102 min.

Little Man Tate (1991). Story centers around a seven-year-old prodigy and his mother. Orion. 99 min.

Mac and Me (1988). Fun adventures between boy and alien. Use of a wheelchair handled sensitively. Orion. 99 min.

One Hundred and One Dalmatians (1961). Adult Dalmatians save ninety-nine pups from Cruella DeVill, a foe who has her heart set on making new fur coats. Disney. 79 min.

The Rescuers Down Under (1990). Mice save animals and a kidnapped boy from an evil hunter. Disney. 74 min.

The Secret of Nimh (1982). Family of mice flees from spring plowing with the help of brilliant lab rats. MGM/United Artists. 82 min.

Sounder (1972). Outstanding film about a loving African-American family during the Depression. Best Picture Nomination. 20th Century Fox. 105 min.

·5·

The Gift of Humor

Humor adds color to a world
gone grey with inattention. [41]

Anne Wilson Schael,
American writer

Is humor a gift?

Webster's Dictionary defines humor as "the quality that makes something seem funny, amusing, or ludicrous."[42] But it is much more than that. Of all the gifts discussed in this book, humor is the one that has the most wide-ranging power. When used appropriately, it can bring you to laughter, make you feel good, or relieve anxiety. It can even repair misunderstandings, spark romance, motivate a learner, increase attention, improve physical well-being, foster friendships, and make even the dullest subject more interesting. What's amazing is that many people do not appreciate how precious and desirable this gift is in children. Let's take a closer look at this complex treasure and its three basic components: **comprehension, production,** and **appreciation.**[43]

Comprehension is clearly crucial to humor. Obviously, an individual needs to understand a riddle in order to find it funny. Likewise, there must be the realization that a situation is absurd before it can strike one's funny bone. By examining the prerequisites to comprehending different types of humor, we can see the many variables that are involved.

Why didn't the skeleton cross the road?
Because he didn't have the guts.

Funny? Maybe, or maybe not—to you. It's probably very funny to Kenji, your typical fifth grader. In order for him to understand this seemingly simple joke, Kenji must have conquered the following subskills:

- the knowledge of the meaning of the words used
- an understanding of the linguistic structure of the verbal interchange (When a question is asked, an answer will follow.)

- the knowledge of the history of the "chicken crossing the road" jokes
- the realization that the word *guts* is used as a pun, meaning both "an organ" and "courage"
- the knowledge of certain facts (Skeletons don't walk and they don't have guts.)
- an understanding that this particular joke consists of an implicit social contract between the joke teller and the listener (I ask you a question. You say, "I don't know." Then I give you the punchline.)
- the ability to conjure up the visual image of a skeleton crossing the street

Now you'll probably never think of a joke in quite the same way! If you think that's complex, wait until you see how much more is required when a joke is presented in the visual form of a comic strip:

In addition to many of the previously mentioned factors, the following subskills are needed to fully process and comprehend this comic strip:

- the ability to sequence events
- the knowledge that the "payoff" will be found in the last panel
- the ability to integrate written and visual stimuli
- the ability to visually discriminate (For example, in the first panel a clock on the wall shows 6:00, in the third panel the clock shows 7:15.)
- in the case of an ongoing and familiar comic strip, knowledge of the history (roles, expectations) of the characters in the strip

Whew! Finally, let's examine a cartoon.

**WHAT HEAVEN WOULD LOOK LIKE
IF GOD WERE A TEN-YEAR-OLD CHILD**

Researchers conclude that the ability to understand a cartoon is an example of problem solving: "In order to construe a cartoon as humorous, the perceiver must recognize the incongruity (punchline/caption) and then be motivated to resolve the incongruity. Resolving the incongruity can be accomplished by one of two means: either retrieving the information from the joke/cartoon or retrieving similar information from one's own experience."[44]

The comprehension of humor is dependent on and influenced by a combination of variables. A perusal of the above examples indicates that not only intellectual ability but also developmental level, social knowledge, temperament, verbal skills, cultural values, and language comprehension all come into play. A child has to have reached a certain level of intellectual and social development to understand different types of humor.

Production is the second aspect of humor. It pertains to how humor is created and used. The pragmatics of humor enters the picture here. The linguistic term **pragmatics** refers to the communicative function of a communicative act. How is humor used in social situations? What is its purpose? Things get a little tricky here.

One important factor concerns the intent of the dispenser of the humor. A person who uses humor successfully must be aware of her or his intent in creating and sharing the humor. Does she or he want to surprise someone, shock them, or catch them off guard? Successful production of humor is based on that which achieves its intended purpose.

Another pertinent factor centers around the social context in which the act of humor takes place. An individual must be aware of the social demands of the particular situation. For example, one joke may be appropriate to share with a friend on the playground, but that same joke may be quite inappropriate to tell someone at a funeral or during a spelling test.

The third factor is dependent on the recipient of the humor. A person who uses humor successfully must be sensitive to the feelings, expectations, and general cognitive level of the recipient. He or she must be prepared for the probable effect that the humor will have on the other person, as well as be able to anticipate its likely consequences. A story may come off as funny to one listener but offensive to another. After reading a cartoon, one person may roll her eyes and clearly appreciate the humor, while another may roll his eyes and communicate displeasure. A person of limited intellectual ability or verbal skills may need a joke, riddle, or cartoon modified in order to understand it, whereas a person of higher intellectual ability will be able to comprehend the joke given more complicated language. Sensitivity to subtle verbal and nonverbal cues, then, is crucial to the successful creation of humor.

> **Did you know?**
> When you laugh, natural pain relievers are released in your body. [45]

The final component of humor is **appreciation**. Some children value being the recipient or dispenser of humorous acts. They enjoy these interactions and seek them out with relish. Perhaps your child is one of those lucky people.

Is your child particularly strong in the area of humor?

Elementary-age children are notorious for their love of jokes, riddles, puns, and humorous stories, especially during the middle and later elementary years. They seem to naturally appreciate the enjoyment and power of humor at this developmental stage. Yet even within this group there are children who are especially adept in this area. Let's return to our friend Kenji. Here are some questions you may want to ask to assess whether humor is a particularly strong gift or talent for him, beginning with the most obvious:

- Does Kenji make you laugh often?
- Does he laugh often?
- Does he like to tell jokes or riddles?
- Does he use puns?
- Does he have an uncanny ability to notice the absurdity or irony in certain situations?
- Does he use humor successfully to escape a tense or uncomfortable moment?
- Does he encourage humor in others?
- Do other people describe him as funny, a goofball, a clown, or a "real character"?
- Does he seem to try to catch you off guard with unusual or silly questions?
- Does he inject humor into his school assignments (for example, funny drawings in the margins; smiling faces to dot his *i*s; outlandish characters, names, titles, or plots in his stories)?
- Does he enjoy reading joke books or the comics in the newspaper?
- Does he like to draw cartoons?
- Does he seem to find humor in serious situations?

Like leadership, there are different styles of humor. Let's say you have two children, Jessica and David. Jessica is quite the extrovert. She seems to be chattering all the time and has loads of friends. Her laughter often fills your home and is boisterous and infectious. In your mind, she has a strong sense of humor.

David is a quiet child with few friends. His laugh is best described as a gentle giggle. At first you may think humor does not play a particularly important role in his life.

Don't be deceived. David may possess a solid comprehension of humor, as well as a strong ability in its production and appreciation. His qualities, however, are hidden. They are not as salient as his sister's. David may create humor in a subtle manner through his writings or his drawings. Perhaps he doesn't volunteer to share his humorous attempts, preferring to keep them to himself, while Jessica, because of her effective verbal skills and personality, may manifest her humor with jokes and outrageous anecdotes.

As discussed in Chapter One, try to observe your child objectively without judgment and preconceived ideas. Jot down in a notebook instances of humor evidenced by your youngster. You might have the next Nora Ephron, Norman Cousins, or Jerry Seinfeld in front of you and not be aware of it!

How to help your child develop her or his humorous side.

One of the most enjoyable ways for you to encourage humor in your child is to let yourself be the object, as well as a source, of humor. Loosen up. There's no need to be serious *all* the time. Do you point out the absurdity of some situations? Do you enjoy a good laugh? Do you allow yourself to look foolish once in a while? Do you laugh at your own mistakes? Again, you are your child's best teacher.

Talk about humor with your youngster. Ask your daughter or son if anything funny happened at school. Discuss what is shared. Talk about what made the situation funny. Point out the benefits of humor. Did the guest speaker's jokes make the presentation more interesting? Did the cartoon the teacher placed in the middle of the test make the experience more fun?

Discuss how humor can be used to deal with difficult situations and to get across serious points of view. Use an example such as:

A poster in a public building read:
"If you must smoke, do not exhale."[46]

Encourage your child to find more examples. Analyze them over dinner. Is the serious message lost in the humor, or does the humor draw attention to the message and make it more palpable?

One topic you can discuss with your middle and upper elementary school-age child is the difference between jokes and humor. Humes describes this difference in the following manner:

> **Humor is a social lubricant that helps us get over some of the bad spots.** [47]
>
> Steve Allen,
> *American humorist, writer, and musician*

"A joke is verbal slapstick—it lacks both build-up and believability. It doesn't come out of your own experience. It has been manufactured, not tailor-fit to your occasion…Humor flows out of the person or the moment. Humor builds suspense and tension, then releases it, sometimes by presenting the unexpected or the familiar in an unfamiliar context. It is the flash anticipation or sudden insight by the audience that triggers laughter. Humor is build-up, bomb, and burst."[48]

> **Aristotle described humor as "the pleasurable distortion of what is expected."** [49]

Play with the distinction between humor and jokes. Give examples of various jokes and humorous situations. See if your child can do the same. An added benefit to this exercise is that you are helping your child develop her or his critical thinking skills, as well as sharpening your youngster's abilities in the area of humor.

**An example of the importance of
"the unexpected" in a humorous story:**

Stanford University researchers ended a long-standing debate among owl specialists as to which sense owls rely on most to detect food at night. In a journal article, they concluded "sight" to be most important after conducting an experiment in which owls were fitted with eyeglasses.[50]

Reinforce your child's attempts at humor. Laugh at what is funny. Thank your child for lightening up a tense moment. Share the humor with other family members or a neighbor.

As discussed in Chapter Three, you'll also want to encourage the process rather than just praise the final product. It is best to encourage your child's humorous attempt, whether or not it is successful, as opposed to merely praising your child for being funny. In doing so, you avoid the pitfall of implying that your love and acceptance are dependent on your child's being successful. Furthermore, you encourage your child to take chances. For example, saying "I've never heard that pun used before," "Your cartoons are showing some good thinking," or "You're making terrific progress in how you end your stories" will foster risk taking, self-evaluation, and persistence, qualities that are necessary for your youngster to develop to her or his fullest potential.[51]

Teach your child the difference between good humor and bad humor. Adults are usually able to differentiate between complex types of humor, such as satire and black humor. Because of their developmental level, however, children in the elementary years have a more difficult time distinguishing one type of humor from another. That's why it is best at this stage to clearly differentiate between healthy and positive humor and its opposite, which is hurtful and negative humor.[52] Good humor can be defined as follows:

- It is life-affirming.
- It doesn't put down or denigrate people from other cultures or those who have differences.
- It doesn't use foul language.
- It leaves all parties in the transaction feeling positive.
- No one's feelings are hurt.
- It doesn't humiliate others.
- It is not mean-spirited.
- You wouldn't mind being the recipient of the humor.
- No one feels left out.

Bad humor can be described as the opposite:

- It is used to put down or denigrate people from other cultures or those who have differences.
- It uses foul language.
- It leaves someone feeling bad.
- Someone's feelings are hurt.
- It is used to humiliate someone.
- It is mean-spirited.
- You would dislike being the recipient of the humor.
- Someone feels left out; he or she is not "in" on the joke.

A word of caution: When you find your child using bad humor, remember that your goal is to change the *form* of the humor. You do not want to discourage the underlying *attempt* at humor. Feedback should be gentle and specific. "How do you think that makes Malcolm feel?" "Can you think of another way to pull this prank so that Malcolm won't feel left out?" These types of questions will help your child differentiate between good and bad humor. They will also assist your youngster in problem solving and help her or him realize the advantages and disadvantages of each type of humor.

Suggested Activities
That Foster Humor

- **Clip funny stories, headlines, and ads from newspapers and magazines.** Put them in a special shoebox. Encourage your child to do the same. On a day when your child is home sick from school, or on a rainy day, pull out the shoeboxes and share the contents of them with each other.

- Does your child get impatient while waiting in line with you at the grocery store? **Ask a goofy question** like, "What would you do if you woke up tomorrow and found that your hair had turned to cotton candy?" You'll be amazed how quickly your child's mood will shift.

- **Make one day a month "silly meal day."** Serve dishes that are weird and outrageous, like porcupine dessert (a pear half with protruding licorice sticks) or snake stew (where every ingredient has a long, thin shape). Serve your meal backward, starting with dessert. Encourage your child to help create the menu.

- Traditions are a wonderful way to connect the many aspects of life that make up your family. **Encourage your child to collect humorous anecdotes from your family's day-to-day experiences.** Start a tradition where these anecdotes are shared on a special day each year. Perhaps a birthday or New Year's Eve may be the designated day. An added bonus is that this activity is a great way to keep a log of your child's development.

• **Ask your youngster to think of all the words or phrases that describe how people respond to something that is funny.** Thurston and Lundberg[53] list over twenty. See if your child can come up with these and others.

laugh	snicker
chuckle	be in stitches
roar	titter
grin	roll in the aisles
smile	crack up
smirk	guffaw
chortle	giggle
beam	shriek
break up	snort
howl	cackle

• **Change the words of familiar songs to create nonsense songs.** Sing your masterpieces before meals.

• **If you have several children, have them trade places and be each other for an hour or two.** Encourage them to trade names, personalities, tastes in food, vocabularies, even television preferences. This is guaranteed to bring not only much laughter and a good time for all, but also a chance to creatively experiment with empathy.

• Don't wait for Halloween to dress up in costumes. **Proclaim a mini-Halloween night one evening.** Have every member of the family dress in costumes, put on wild makeup, and wear masks. (You, too!) Take pictures of everyone.

- **Have your child help you collect silly songs** (for example, Bobby McFerrin's "Don't Worry, Be Happy"). Record them onto a cassette tape. Pull out the tape when you need to lighten up a tense moment or fill some time while waiting. You'll be impressed by the magic of music.

- Need an activity when several of your child's friends are over to play? Give each child an old magazine and scissors. Ask each to cut out about six or eight pictures. On separate slips of paper, **have each child make up an amusing caption for each picture**. Then have the children share their projects. Everyone tries to guess which caption goes with which picture. Encourage them to be silly.

- **Take your child on a guided imagery adventure** to a faraway fantasy place to meet a famous funny person (how about Bart Simpson?) or to solve a silly dilemma. Be sure you and your youngster are relaxed beforehand, with your eyes closed, and with quiet music or gentle sounds in the background. Share your adventures with each other. This activity helps teach your child that humor can be gentle and quiet; it doesn't need to be wild and loud.

- **Suggest that the family have a "collect a joke" day.** Every member should collect jokes from friends, teachers, and colleagues during the day. In the evening, share the goodies.

Make your home a place where humor is evident. If you find a particularly funny cartoon, attach it to the refrigerator. Are funny reading materials readily available? Is there a goofy photograph that is sure to evoke a smile? A home filled with laughter is one where individuals feel free to make mistakes, where creativity flourishes, and where family members want to be. It also helps breed family interaction. Be sure your home is filled with laughter. Happy times will follow for you and your family.

Ask yourself: Isn't it more pleasant to be around people with a sense of humor than those without? If your child has the gift of humor, you are a lucky parent indeed. Humor adds a wonderful dimension to your child's development and to your family life as a whole. It is a gift that deserves to be nurtured. Enjoy the laughter!

A Conversation About Humor

What better way to understand the importance of humor than to talk with one of our country's leading humorists, **Steve Allen**? Among his many accomplishments, Steve was the originator and first host of "The Tonight Show," the star of the long-running and critically acclaimed "The Steve Allen Comedy Hour," and the creator, writer, and host of the Emmy award-winning PBS-TV series "Meeting of Minds." He has written more than forty books, including *How to Be Funny* and *Make Them Laugh*. He has composed almost five thousand songs, plus the scores for several musicals, and starred on Broadway and in motion pictures. In the spring of 1994 the Museum of Television and Radio honored him with a three-month retrospective of his work. Comedian, writer, musician, philosopher—Steve Allen is truly a gifted individual.

Q: *Do you think humor is a gift?*

A: Yes. There is such a thing as a gift for humor, just as there is for music, athletic, or mathematical abilities.... It does not follow that only those so genetically gifted can practice these particular disciplines. I think the tricks of the trade can be taught. I have never met anyone who I would describe as totally humorless. There are some people who don't seem to have much of that ability, and there are other people who are sourpusses. But even the sourpusses often are seen to laugh and smile, so there must be something that strikes them funny...It's an endless universe, because unlike music, which is concerned with nuts and bolts, details, violins, piano strings, and drumheads and that sort of thing, humor isn't essentially connected with anything concrete at all. You can't hold a pound of humor in your hand. But it's a matter of reacting to human experience, whether that experience is direct or a matter of verbal communication. And I think it is part of our evolutionary endowment...because we have actual musculature and nervous equipment by means of which we perform those two physical acts called smiling and laughing. Just as we do other acts, like running, breathing, sweating, and so forth. So to me that shows that humor is not some very late add-on, but is intimately connected with the essence of human nature.

Q: *Do you think humor can be encouraged in children?*

A: Yes. The gift of humor is found in all children...[they] seem to show a clear playfulness especially in the first few years.... There's no doubt that all children have that, but it sometimes gets discouraged in them by adults, parents who try to get children to "stop that." I don't think anybody ever tries to stop it totally, but on the other hand it ought to be encouraged, not stopped. Children have to be taught that there are times and places where playfulness is not appropriate. You wouldn't approve if your child ran into a funeral, for example, and began to act up or try to be cute. But with the exception of such rare instances, it's one of the glorious things about childhood.... So starting with that gift, which apparently is in all children...it should be relatively easy for aware parents and teachers, within boundaries, within limitations, to encourage that natural human gift...and yet channel it in appropriate directions.

Q: *Can you think of some specific ways that parents can encourage humor in their children?*

A: There are thousands of books that are ideal for that purpose...the Dr. Seuss books, for example. There are many examples of works that are designed not only to entertain children, but to enlighten them, to amuse them, to make them laugh. This can be done by the text, or by the pictures, or both, which is usually the case. So that is one answer to your question.

Then I think it wouldn't do the parents in most homes any harm to lighten up a little bit.... You can learn to take a philosophical look at life.... The raw material of comedy is tragedy.... We never joke about the sweet stuff, like cotton candy. We joke about funerals, death, people going to talk to St. Peter...disease, war....

Humor is one of the means...of not being steamrolled by the truly tragic aspects of the human predicament....This is a very difficult planet to live on, and if we ourselves survive reasonably unscathed, we can see just by looking across the street, or on the evening news, or reading the afternoon newspaper, that literally millions daily do not have such luck.

Q: *How has humor helped you in your life, other than in your career, which is obvious?*

A: It's the same way it helps everyone.... In my own life there have been many instances, perhaps even daily instances, in which the ability to perceive the humorous element in a situation was helpful.... I think in the lives of almost everyone, they tend unconsciously, automatically, to use humor in some kind of a defensive or self-protective way.

Humor is a real fortunate blessing, again whether it's somehow endowed by a great Creator, or just one of those weird accidents of nature, we don't really know. But it is something without which life would be much more unpleasant than it is.

Q: *Laughter sure is contagious, isn't it?*

A: Yes. Laughter has in common with yawning that contagious factor. It's catching...Laughter is, among other things, a social exercise.

Where to Go for More Information on Humor

Allen, S., with J. Woolman (1987). *How to Be Funny*. New York: McGraw-Hill.

Communication Aids for Children and Adults (1994). Adapted toys for children with special needs.

Crestwood Co.
6625 N. Sidney Pl.
Milwaukee, WI 53209-3259
(414) 352-5678
FAX: (414) 352-5679

Humes, J. C. (1975). *Podium Humor: A Raconteur's Treasury of Witty and Humorous Stories*. New York: HarperCollins.

Johnson, E. W. (1994). *A Treasury of Humor II*. New York: Ivy/Ballantine Books.

Rovin, J. (1991). *1,001 Great Sports Jokes*. New York: Penguin. This is not a children's book, so some of the jokes will go over your child's head. However, recommended for sports buffs of all ages.

The Successful Student Catalog (1994). "What's wrong?" cards: humorous flash cards depicting absurd scenes to make children think.
The Center for Applied Psychology, Inc.
P.O. Box 61586
King of Prussia, PA 19406
(800) 67-STUDY
FAX: 610-277-4556

Thurston, C. M. & E. M. Lundberg (1992). *If They're Laughing, They're Not Killing Each Other: Ideas for Using Humor Effectively in the Classroom Even If You're Not Funny Yourself*. Fort Collins, Colo.: Cottonwood Press. Geared for teachers, but some wonderful ideas for parents, too.

Walker, B. K. Illustrated by Simms Taback (1992). *Laughing Together: Giggles and Grins from Around the Globe*. Minneapolis: Free Spirit Publishing. Directed toward parents and teachers but may readily be used by children grades 3 and up.

Children's Books That Encourage Humor

Berger, M. Illustrated by R. Mujica (1989). *101 Wacky Science Jokes*. New York: Scholastic (grades 2–6). Also available are collections of president jokes and state jokes.

Berk, M. & T. Vavrus. Illustrated by J. Sinclair (1992). *Go Ahead—Make Me Laugh*. New York: Sterling (grades 2–6). Tongue-twisters, riddles, and more.

Maddocks, P. (1992). *Cartooning for Beginners: A Step-By-Step Guide to Drawing Cartoons*. London: O'Mara Books Limited (grades 2 and up). Fun approach; follow-up to a previous book on cartooning by author.

Miller, L. M. Illustrated by S. Hoffman (1990). *Shake, Riddle & Roll*. New York: Sterling (grades 2–6). Goofy riddles.

Rosen, M. Illustrated by M. Brown (1994). *Off the Wall: A Very Silly Storybook*. New York: Kingfisher Books (grades 2–6). Over twenty-five very silly stories.

Solga, K. (1992). *Make Clothes Fun! Art and Activities for Kids*. Cincinnati: North Light Books/F&W Publ., Inc. (grades 1 and up). Clear directions for ten art projects, including goofy hats and buttoned, decorated T-shirts.

Watterson, B. (1993). *The Days Are Just Packed*. Kansas City: Universal Press Syndicate. One of a series of compilations of Calvin and Hobbes comic strips. Enjoyed by adults and children alike.

•6•

Answers to Common Questions About Gifts, Talents, and Interests

To maintain a joyful family requires much from both the parents and the children. Each member of the family has to become, in a special way, the servant of the others. [54]

Pope John Paul II,
leader of the Catholic Church

The following questions and answers are intended to explore some of the problem areas and difficulties that parents sometimes face when dealing with their children's gifts, talents, and interests.

Q: *What if I've observed my child but still don't see any particular strengths in the areas of leadership, creativity, social consciousness, or humor?*

A: There are many types of gifts, talents, and special interest areas. The ones discussed in this book are just four examples. Keep observing your child. Continue exposing your youngster to new types of activities. You never know what will strike your daughter or son's fancy. Other gifts, talents, and areas of strength that you may want to look for are

- the ability to make friends
- mathematical problem solving
- peacemaking
- interest in how the human body works
- negotiating
- building structures
- computer work
- high energy (Believe it or not, it is a gift!)
- organization
- spirituality
- passion for history
- interest in fashion
- love of photography
- high task commitment
- knack for storytelling

• athletic ability
• skill in writing.

Q: *How can you tell when areas of interest are inappropriate?*

A: There is a popular notion among educators and psychologists called "goodness of fit."[55] The "fit" refers to how well the inclinations, competencies, and temperament of a child match the demands of the different social environments that make up that child's world. Families, classrooms, and peer play groups are examples of social environments.

Your child may have an interest area that is inappropriate for her or his particular family, classroom, or friends. We'll call this "inappropriate" with a small *i*. Most interests that are inappropriate fall into this category. Your family might consider an interest in fashion to be a frivolous and useless endeavor, while another family may find it quite fascinating. One group of friends may be completely uninterested in fashion, while another may share your child's interest.

You need to ask yourself: Is my child's interest inappropriate simply because it doesn't match the interests of the rest of the family and the child's peers? If so, then you might want to consider how you can open up your family to be more responsive to your child's particular area of strength, as well as introduce your child to like-minded children.

Some areas of interest are inappropriate in a more serious way. We'll call this "Inappropriate" with a capital *I*.

These are areas of interest that stand out as being weird, bizarre, or seriously gender- or age-inappropriate. An eight-year-old with a strong interest in pornography, methods of torture, disease, or the like may need to be assessed by a family doctor or school psychologist. Such interests may be a sign of a potentially serious psychological problem.

Another way that gifts, talents, and interests can be Inappropriate is if they are so extreme that they interfere with your child's normal day-to-day functioning. When a child becomes singularly focused on a particular area of interest, other parts of that child's life may become negatively affected. Friends may stop coming around; school performance may slip. Family members may notice that the child is spending increasingly long periods of time in isolation. Most often, these obsessive interests fade away on their own. However, if this behavior persists over several months, an evaluation by a family doctor or school psychologist may be in order. Otherwise, let your child be interested in what comes naturally to her or him. Allow for differences and individuality.

Q: *You talk about humor as a gift. What do I do if my little boy has absolutely no sense of humor?*

A: If this is the only unusual characteristic you see in your son, then there is probably no need to worry. This may simply be a reflection of his temperament or personality.

There are exceptions, however. If your child rarely laughs or smiles in response to jokes or humorous situations that other children tend to find amusing, you may be confronted by a serious problem. A greatly restricted sense of humor is often symptomatic of childhood depression, because depressed children are less capable of responding to humor than nondepressed children.[56]

Depression is a *syndrome* that shows up as a combination of behaviors, a "package," so to speak. If your child manifests several of the characteristics below a few hours a day over several weeks or months, and if the characteristics do not appear to be logically tied to environmental events, then it is recommended that you speak to your child's pediatrician, school special educator, or school psychologist. Some children have alternating periods of depressed and nondepressed moods, so it is advised that you document your child's behavior by keeping notes on times and dates of moods, relevant statements, and so forth.

Children who suffer from depression can be helped. If you have suspicions in this area, act now.

Warning Signs of Childhood Depression
Adapted from Stark[57] and DSM-III-R[58]

♦ a sad mood, often described as feeling "down," "bad," "yucky," or "empty"

♦ a loss of pleasure from activities or events that used to be enjoyed

♦ an angry or irritable mood

♦ social withdrawal

♦ fatigue or hyperactivity

♦ low response to humor

♦ difficulty in school

♦ sleeping problems

♦ eating problems

♦ talk of suicide or wishing to be dead

♦ negative self-evaluations

♦ feelings of hopelessness

♦ persistent aches and pains

♦ a marked change in normal behavior

Q: *How do I handle extreme or weird interest areas?*

A: One effective way to handle excessive or inappropriate interests is to try to shape your child's interest into a more appropriate area.

Let's use an example mentioned earlier of disease. Your child, Andrew, seems obsessed with this topic. He reads about it, draws pictures of what he thinks disease looks like, and talks about the subject every chance he gets. Friends are avoiding him. You're worried.

First, meet him on his level. Talk with your son about exactly what interests him, for example, disease in animals. Then start to interject a related, more appropriate side topic, such as other interesting facts about animals or differences between two species in terms of their eating habits.

You'll want to make these new side topics functionally reinforcing for your child. Remember the discussion concerning reinforcement in Chapter Three? In one of his homework assignments, point out how Andrew can use a difference between two famous leaders in terms of their accomplishments. Share a fun activity that centers around one of your side topics. Sometimes a gentle shaping or redirecting of an interest pattern is effective in dealing with an inappropriate situation.

Another suggestion is to take a look at Andrew's environment. Is he being stimulated and challenged at school? Is your home a generally loving and happy place to be? Is Andrew going through a particularly difficult time right now? Does his teacher report that he manifests his obsession in school? You may find that the answers to these questions will point you in the direction of a solution.

Most important, seek help if the problem persists. Childhood is too precious a time to waste.

Q: *My daughter, Kate, has a strong interest in social areas, like helping others and getting involved. Unfortunately, she is reading a year behind most of her classmates. Is there any way I can use her particular gift to improve her area of weakness?*

A: Provide Kate with "low reading level, high interest" materials in her area of interest. Give her opportunities to read about people who contributed successfully to social causes and what children can do to help the world. Ask her teacher what materials are available at school that would serve this function. There are dozens of companies that offer such educational materials. Most schools have a number of their catalogs on hand that you can browse through. Ask Kate's teacher if it would be possible to order several for the classroom. Order some on your own as a special "I love you" present. Speak to the school or local librarian about what is available that would suit Kate's needs. Your objective is simple: Provide Kate with opportunities to read about what interests her. (Resources for low reading level, high interest materials can be found at the end of this chapter.)

You'll also want to continue supporting Kate's area of interest in ways that do not require reading. Listen to speeches on the subject. Watch television programs together that are related to social concern. Provide your daughter with activities that allow her to practice the skills necessary in this area, such as those described in Chapter Four.

Finally, concentrate on what Kate *can* do. She has a gift in a wonderful area. You should be proud.

Q: *My son is very creative, but he's driving me crazy! His projects are scattered all over the house. Any suggestions?*

A: Children, even creative ones, should not be allowed to infringe on the rights of others. You and the rest of your family have the right to an organized, neat home. Yet it's important that your son have the necessary space to create contraptions and experiment with an assortment of materials.

Why not allocate a particular area of the house for projects? Perhaps the garage, your son's bedroom, or a little-used guest room could be chosen. If you have no such room available in your home, see if you can find at least a small area just for your son. One of the shelves of a bookshelf, part of a closet, or a section of the kitchen cabinets may be just what is needed. This area should be fairly off-limits to the rest of the family, if possible. Encourage your son to finish his projects so that he can make room for more. If the designated area is in shared living quarters, have your son help you generate clear rules about how long projects can be left in this area. Check with your son's teacher to see if there is any room available at his school to display a particular finished project or two.

Q: *Are there any gifts, talents, or interests that are better than others? Should I be steering my daughter in a particular direction?*

A: The answer to both questions is *no*. Your daughter is an individual. Her interests are her own, not yours. Unless the interest is unhealthy, dangerous, or seriously inappropriate, she should be allowed to blossom in those areas which naturally appeal to her.

Resist the temptation to push your daughter in a particular direction. Expose her to many different types of activities: sports, creative writing, performing arts, computers, and so forth. Remember, most gifts and talents have inherent worth. With your encouragement and support, your child will find her "own voice."

◆ ◆ ◆

It is hoped that this book has provided you with both the skills to identify your child's areas of strength and interest and practical ways to nurture those special gifts and talents. The benefits to your child's development will be immense. Best wishes for much success!

21. Arnold, J. E. (1962). "Useful Creative Techniques." In S. J. Parnes & H. F. Harding, *A Source Book for Creative Thinking*. New York: Charles Scribner's Sons.

22. Runco, M. A. (1991). *Divergent Thinking*. Norwood, N.J.: Ablex.

23. Hitz, R. & A. Driscoll. "Praise or Encouragement? New Insights into Praise: Implications for Early Childhood Teachers." *Young Children*, July 1988.

24. Boorstin, D. J. (1992). *The Creators: A History of Heroes of the Imagination*. New York: Random House.

25. Anderson, *Great Quotes from Great Women*.

26. Hoff, T. "HyperCard and Image Processing as Vehicles for Gifted/Talented Students." *The National Research Center on the Gifted and Talented Newsletter*, Winter 1994.

27. Baker, E., M. Gearhart & J. Herman (1990). *Assessment of Apple Classrooms of Tomorrow (ACOT): Evaluation Study of First and Second-Year Findings*. ACOT Report #7: UCLA Center for Technology Assessment. Apple Classrooms of Tomorrow, Advanced Technology Group, Apple Computer.

28. Gardner, H. (1993). *The Creative Mind*. New York: Basic Books.

29. Clark, B. (1986). *Optimizing Learning: The Integrative Model in the Classroom*. Columbus, Ohio: Merrill.

30. Davis, Wynn, ed. (1992). *The Best of Success: A Treasury of Success Ideas*. Lombard, Ill.: Celebrating Excellence.

31. Bandura, A. (1977). *Social Learning Theory*. Englewood Cliffs, N.J.: Prentice Hall.

32. Lamme, L. & L. McKinley. "Creating a Caring Classroom with Children's Literature." *Young Children*. November 1992, 65–71.

33. *Statistical Profile of Special Education in the United States 1994*. Supplement to *Teaching Exceptional Children*, Vol. 26, No. 3, January 1994. (Source: 15th Annual Report to Congress, 1993.)

34. Quicke, J. (1985). *Disability in Modern Children's Fiction*. Cambridge, Mass.: Brookline Books.

35. National Wildlife Federation (1989). *National Wildlife*. June–July.

36. Shaw, G. B. (1932). "Adventures of the Black Girl in Her Search for God." In E. Weintraub (1977), *The Portable Bernard Shaw*. New York: Viking Penguin.

37. Jackson, W. (1990). "Wrong Assumptions and the Patterns They Impose." In J. Rifkin (ed.), *The Green Lifestyle Handbook*. New York: Holt & Co.

38. Appelhof, M. (1982). *Worms Eat My Garbage*. Kalamazoo, Mich.: Flower Press.

39. Johns, F. D., K. A. Liske & A. L. Evans (1986). *Education Goes Outdoors*. Menlo Park, Calif.: Addison-Wesley.

40. Lewis, B. A. (1991). *The Kid's Guide to Social Action*. Minneapolis: Free Spirit.

41. Schael, A. W. (1990). *Meditations for Women Who Do Too Much*. San Francisco: Harper.

42. *Webster's New World Dictionary* (1982). 2nd College Edition. New York: Simon & Schuster.

43. Ziv, A. (1984). *Personality and a Sense of Humor*. New York: Springer.

44. Short, E. J., L. A. Basili & C. W. Schatschneider. "Analysis of Humor Skills Among Elementary School Students: Comparisons of Children With and Without Intellectual Handicaps." *American Journal of Mental Retardation* 98, 1, 63–73, 1993.

45. Klein, A. (1989). *The Healing Power of Humor*. Los Angeles: Jeremy P. Tarcher.

46. Johnson, E. W. (1994). *A Treasury of Humor II*. New York: Ivy/Ballantine Books.

47. Allen, S., with J. Woolman (1987). *How to Be Funny*. New York: McGraw-Hill.

48. Humes, J. C. (1985). *Podium Humor: A Raconteur's Treasury of Witty and Humorous Stories*. New York: HarperCollins.

49. Humes, *Podium Humor*.

50. Shepherd, C., J. J. Kohut & R. Sweet (1991). *Beyond News of the Weird*. New York: Plume/Penguin.

51. Smutny, J. F., K. Veenker & S. Veenker (1989). *Your Gifted Child: How to Recognize and Develop the Special Talents in Your Child from Birth to Age Seven*. New York: Ballantine Books.

52. Thurston, C. M. & E. M. Lundberg (1992). *If They're Laughing, They're Not Killing Each Other: Ideas for Using Humor Effectively in the Classroom Even if You're Not Funny Yourself*. Fort Collins, Colo.: Cottonwood Press.

53. Thurston & Lundberg, *If They're Laughing*.

54. Anderson, *Great Quotes from Great Leaders*.

55. Keogh, B. (1986). "Temperament and Schooling: Meaning of 'Goodness of Fit.'" In J. Lerner & R. Lerner (eds.), *Temperament and Social Interactions During Infancy and Childhood*. San Francisco: Jossey-Bass.

56. Stark, K. (1990). *Childhood Depression: School-Based Intervention*. The Guilford School Practitioner Series. New York: The Guilford Press.

57. Stark, *Childhood Depression*.

58. American Psychiatric Association (1987). *Diagnostic and Statistical Manual of Mental Disorders* (3rd ed., rev.). Washington, DC: Author.

Other GIFTED & TALENTED® *books that will help*

develop your child's gifts and talents

Workbooks:

Over 5 million sold!

- Reading (4-6) $3.95
- Math (4-6) $3.95
- Language Arts (4-6) $3.95
- Puzzles & Games
  for Reading and Math (4-6) $3.95
- Puzzles & Games for Critical and
  Creative Thinking (4-6) $3.95

- Reading (6-8) $3.95
- Math (6-8) $3.95
- Language Arts (6-8) $3.95
- Puzzles & Games
  for Reading and Math (6-8) $3.95
- Puzzles & Games for Critical and
  Creative Thinking (6-8) $3.95

Reference Workbooks:

- Word Book (4-6) $3.95
- Dictionary (6-8) $3.95

Readers:

- Double the Trouble (6-8) $7.95
- Time for Bed! (6-8) $7.95

Drawing Books:

- Learn to Draw (6 and up) $5.95

For Parents:

- How to Develop Your Child's Gifts
  and Talents During the Elementary
  Years $11.95

Available where good books are sold! **or**
Send a check or money order, plus shipping charges, to:

Department VHG
Lowell House
2029 Century Park East, Suite 3290
Los Angeles, CA 90067

For special or bulk sales, call (800) 552-7551, EXT 112

Note: Minimum order of three titles. **On a separate piece of paper,** please specify exact titles and ages and include a breakdown of costs.

Handy Worksheet

(*# of books*) _____	x $3.95	=	_____
(*# of books*) _____	x $5.95	=	_____
(*# of books*) _____	x $7.95	=	_____
(*# of books*) _____	x $11.95	=	_____
Subtotal		=	_____
California residents add 8.25% sales tax			_____
Shipping charges			
(*# of books*) ____ x $.80/ book		=	_____
Total cost		=	_____